Mudroot Pickles' Big Adventures

Collection of short stories for children

By

Caroline George

This is a work of fiction. Names, characters, incidents or places are a product of the authors imagination or used fictitiously. Any resemblance to actual persons, living or dead, is entirely coincidental.

ISBN: 9798865932154
Imprint: Independently published

These short stories are also published as single stories available on Amazon Kindle.

Cover design by Pixabay / Canva / Amazon KDP

Acknowledgements

Big thanks to the generous community of children's writers for their advice and support along the way. Thanks also to the artists on Pixabay and Canva who provided their artwork on a free to use basis. Final thanks to my ever patient husband who loses his wife for days.

Thank you.

Contents

Page

Mudroot Pickles & His Magic Pickle Stick

by

Caroline George

If you walk down to the bottom of the curious cabbage patch at the end of Crickleberry Lane and past the crooked house with the bright yellow door, you might find your way to Crickleberry Town. You have to look very, very carefully. You have to walk past Rainbow Park with the silly slide and the wonky swings. But, if you get to the candy floss fence and turn right by the first licorice lamp post, you might meet Mudroot Pickles and his friends.

*

Mudroot Pickles is the big cheese in Crickleberry town. He has a booming voice that is loud enough to make the trees shake. Mudroot is only as tall as a rugby ball but what he lacks in height, he makes up for with his big smiley, super white false teeth. If you listen, really, really hard, you might hear a rumble or a roar. Not from a lion who might make you **JUMP**, but from Mudroot Pickles himself, roaring through Crickleberry Town on his motorbike. If you have ever heard Mudroot on his motorbike, roaring down the street, you will have seen the mess he leaves behind as he knocks into bins, spilling old cabbage and sweet wrappers across the path and into the road. Mudroot Pickles may be very clumsy but he has the biggest, kindest heart in the world.

*

As the big cheese in Crickleberry Town, Mudroot Pickles is the best dressed hedgehog. He wears a bright white shirt with a bow tie and a pair of trousers held up with a gold tasseled string. Mudroot loves his bow ties and has matching socks, big and sloppy, that wrinkled over his hairy ankles. Because Mudroot is a very important hedgehog, he wears thick rimmed spectacles and has a brightly coloured waistcoat where he keeps Brian, his shouty silver pocket watch. Brian shouts out the time to Mudroot whenever the clock strikes the hour. Sometimes, Brian can be grumpy, especially if Mudroot disturbs him to ask for the time. Grumpy old Brian!

ITS TEN O CLOCK MUDROOT!

Brian stretched out his arms and shouted out, making Mudroot jump. Mudroot fell backwards onto his fat bottom and let out a loud fart.

TURRUMMP!

'Oops!' Mudroot picked himself up and dusted down his clothes, wondering where on earth that silly noise was coming from. It certainly wasn't from him.

*

Mudroot was busy in his hut folding away his laundry. As he lifted up two pairs of stripey socks, dangling in front of his fire, Lily the chocolate spot lion looked at him, pointing to the stick resting over the fire with the last of Mudroot's washing hanging from it.

'What's that, Mudroot?'

'Oh, it's just my pickle stick.' Mudroot lifted it up and waved it in the air a little.

'That's a silly name. What's a pickle stick?' Lily lion giggled.

Mudroot frowned. 'A pickle stick is not something to be laughed at Lily. It has many uses. My pickle stick is not just for drying my socks in front of the fire.' Mudroot smiled. 'I can use my pickle stick to stir soup, or I can paint at school with it.' Mudroot folded his socks, adding them to the small pile of laundry.

'Is that all it can do? Lily lion looked at him. 'My brother Levi said it was a magic pickle stick.' Mudroot smiled, raising his eyebrows. 'Levi told you it was a magic pickle stick did he?'

*

Lily and Levi are not like other lions. They smile a lot and have spots! Not angry red spots like measles, or scratchy, itchy chicken pox, but chocolate button spots; white ones, brown ones, pink ones, yellow ones, all different flavours of chocolate. They are very yummy. If you can do something that's really kind, Levi and Lily might let you choose a chocolate spot, maybe two or three.

*

'Is it a magic pickle stick?' Lily asked again.

'It's a great back scratcher and I can write in the sand when we go to the beach.' Mudroot looked at Lily lion who wanted to hear more. 'At Christmas I set it up on the mantle and hang baubles and tinsel from it and I can use it to prop up my motorbike.'

'And you can use it as a walking stick.' Lily lion looked at him as someone else knocked on Mudroot's front door.

*

Mudroot walked away from his fire and opened his door. It was Lily's brother, Levi the chocolate spot lion.

'Hello Levi.' Mudroot said. 'Are you looking for Lily?'

'Yes. Is she here?'

Mudroot opened his front door and Levi walked inside.

'Hello Levi.' Lily said. 'Mudroot was telling me about his magic pickle stick.'

Levi lion laughed. 'Have you been telling tall tales about your great grandfather Pickles?' Levi looked at his sister. 'Great grandfather Pickles was the one who started all the magic rumours.'

'Is it a magic pickle stick?' Lily asked again.

'Not at all. It's just a stick.' Mudroot winked at Levi lion who was enjoying a warm by the fire.

'If it's just a stick, why does Sebastian the yellow elephant and Buddy blue bear think it is a magic pickle stick?' Lily looked puzzled.

*

Mudroot reached over to the fire to lift up the pickle stick. He looked at Lily.

'Does it look like a magic pickle stick to you?' Lily ran her fingers over the yellow stick. 'No. It's just a yellow stick.'

'Are you sure? 'Look a little closer Lily.' Mudroot smiled.

Lily the chocolate spot lion looked at the stick. It had been painted in bright yellow paint and had the word **PICKLE** carved out on one side. She looked at one end of the stick. It was painted red. She looked closer and smiled. There was something there, something different. The top of the stick looked as if it had two small wooden hands clasped together at the top.

'These look like little hands.' Lily pointed to the top of the pickle stick.

'Great grandfather Pickles called them helping hands. Here, if you pull the thumb ever so gently.' Mudroot pulled at the thumb at the top of the pickle stick.

To Lily's delight, two little hands opened up to reveal a small but secret hidey hole. Lily stuck her tiny claw inside the end. It wasn't a very big hidey hole but you could definitely put something inside it.

'It doesn't look like magic to me and the helping hands are not very big.' Lily said.

'I'm not very big either but I am big enough.' Mudroot puffed out his chest.

'What is the secret space for?' Lily asked.

‘Well, for great grandfather Pickles it was for something very magical indeed. Let me tell you the story of how great grandfather Pickles saved Crickleberry Town.

*

Inside Mudroot’s waistcoat pocket, Brian let out a grumbling snore that shook the pans hanging in Mudroot’s kitchen. Brian stretched out his arms and shouted.

ITS ELEVEN O CLOCK MUDROOT! WHERE IS MY SNACK?

Brian makes him jump. Mudroot falls backwards onto his fat bottom and lets out a loud fart.

TURRUMMP!

‘Oops!’ Mudroot picked himself up and dusted down his clothes, wondering where on earth that silly noise was coming from. It certainly wasn’t from him.

‘Where is my snack please, Brian. Remember what we said about good manners.’ Mudroot looked at his pocket watch.

WHERE IS MY SNACK PLEEEEEAZZE MUDROOT.

Brian shouted back.

*

Mudroot handed Brian one of the oatmeal cookies that he liked and looked at his friends.

‘It is time for some dandelion tea and an iced bun from the icky sticky bun bush.’ Mudroot said. ‘Let me fetch a tray and then I will tell you all about great grandfather Pickles and the magic pickle stick.’

*

After tea and buns, Mudroot sat down in his favourite armchair as Lily and Levi curled up by the fire.

‘A very long time ago, my great grandfather Pickles got himself into a little bit of trouble. It was a sunny Sunday in the summer. A very busy day in Crickleberry Town. Great grandfather Pickles was taking some more lemonade bottles to the lemonade fountain. He had a motorbike, very much like mine. His sidecar was so full of bottles that he couldn’t really see where he was going.

*

Great grandfather Pickles always stuck to the back path, where visitors to the town were not supposed to go, so he thought it would be safe.'

'Is that the path that runs behind the old barn? Lily looked at him.

'Yes, that's the path. Anyway, great grandfather Pickles was taking the bottles to the fountain when, out of nowhere, a little boy on a blue tricycle came speeding towards him. Great grandfather Pickles swerved out of the way but the little boy still fell off his bike.'

'What happened to the lemonade bottles?' Lily asked.

'Well, it was such a to do. They bounced out of the side car and rolled onto the grass. Thankfully though, none of them were broken.'

‘That little boy shouldn’t have been on the back path.’ Levi said.

‘I think he might have been lost.’ Mudroot replied.

‘What happened next?’ Lily asked.

*

‘The little boy fell onto the grass and cut his knee. It was just a teeny, tiny, little scratch but there was some blood.’ Mudroot sighed. ‘The little boy made such a big fuss. He was crying and wailing and making such a noise that his parents didn’t know what to do. Great grandfather Pickles offered the little boy some free lemonade and ice cream but he kept on crying.’

‘But everyone knows that ice cream and lemonade helps a sore knee.’ Levi said.

'I know that, you know that and great grandfather Pickles knew that but the little boy would not stop crying.'

'Oh dear.' Lily said.

'Then the little boy's Father, who just happened to be the Mayor, started shouting at great grandfather Pickles. He was very cross.'

'What did the Mayor say?' Lily asked.

'He said that great grandfather Pickles was very silly and that he should have been watching where he was driving. Great grandfather Pickles was very sorry.'

'Was the little boy still crying?' Lily asked.

'Yes. He would not stop. Great grandfather Pickles had to act fast.'

'What did he do?' Lily asked.

'Well, as the story goes, great grandfather Pickles saw that the little boy's mummy was trying to apply some soothing cream onto the little boy's knee, but he was still crying and wailing. The ice cream didn't work, the lemonade didn't work and the soothing cream didn't work, but great grandfather Pickles had something that no one else had.' Mudroot smiled.

'His magic pickle stick.' Lily said.

'Yes, his magic pickle stick.'

'But it's just a stick.' Lily looked at him.

'Who's telling this story?' Mudroot reached for his stick and tapped it on the floor. 'Great grandfather Pickles lifted up his pickle stick and walked over to the little boy. Then he started to chant.'

A little bit of magic

A tiny tap and click

A few quick dabs

With my magic pickle stick.

'Great grandfather Pickles very gently dabbed the end of his pickle stick over the little boys sore knee and a tiny drop of sparkling, glittering cream fell from the pickle stick onto the little boy's knee.' Mudroot clapped his hands. 'Well, that did the trick.'

'Like magic?' Lily sat very still.

'Just like magic.' Mudroot smiled. 'And just like magic the little boy stopped crying.'

'But how did great grandfather Pickles get the sparkling, glittering cream?'

Mudroot pointed to the clasped hands at one end of the pickle stick.

'The hands are so small no one can see them open, and inside the little hidey hole I always have a little bit of magic cream.'

Lily giggled. 'So it's a trick stick not a magic pickle stick?'

'You never know when you might need a little bit of magic and great grandfather Pickles saved the day that summer.'

'The magic pickle stick is more than a pair of helping hands Mudroot.' Levi said. 'Tell Lily about what else it can do.'

'It can keep me out of trouble, that's what.' Mudroot smiled.

'Can it change vegetables into chocolate?' Lily asked.

'No, nothing like that.'

'Can it stop rainy days?'

'No.'

'Can it stop Sybil swirly snake giving me a hug when I don't want one?'

'No.'

'Can it find easter eggs?'

'No but if the Easter bunny was in the area my magic pickle stick might be able to find it.'

Mudroot stood up. 'My pickle stick can always help me make things a little better. That's enough magic for me.'

Brian the silver pocket watch shouted out.

ITS ONE O CLOCK MUDROOT! TIME FOR SOME LUNCH!

Brian makes him jump. Mudroot falls backwards onto his fat bottom and lets out a loud fart.

TURRUMMP!

'Oops!' Mudroot picked himself up and dusted down his clothes, wondering where on earth that silly noise came from. It certainly wasn't from him.

*

'I think that's enough of my magic pickle stick story for today.' Mudroot said.

Levi lion uncurled his tail and stretched out his paws. He licked his lips, picking up the aroma of the tomato soup that was bubbling on the cooker.

'I think I can smell soup.' Levi said.

'Tomato and vegetable soup.' Mudroot replied. 'With a buttered crumpet for dipping.'

Levi licked his lips. 'Sounds lovely.'

'You should both stay.' Mudroot smiled. 'There's plenty to go around.'

*

The friends sat around Mudroot's kitchen table with big bowls of tomato and vegetable soup. There was a stack of toasted crumpets for dipping and thick chocolate custard for pudding. Mudroot was so full of food after lunch that he had to undo the buttons of his waistcoat and have a lie down.

'Ickle fickle what a pickle I can barely move.' Mudroot groaned.

'Thank you for lunch Mudroot.' Levi said. 'It tasted delicious.'

'Thank you for telling me the story about great grandfather Pickles and the magic pickle stick.' Lily said.

'We will leave you to your afternoon nap.' Levi waved goodbye.

*

With Lily and Levi, the chocolate spot lions making their way home, Mudroot Pickles lay down on his bed. He looked at his purple silk Pyjamas wondering if it was too early to put them on.

'What time is it Brian?'

Brian the shouty silver pocket watch stretched out his arms and grumbled.

WHAT DO YOU WANT MUDROOT? IT'S ONLY TWENTY PAST THREE!

It was too early to put his Pyjamas on. Mudroot smiled and looked up at the cobwebs on his ceiling. He had enjoyed his lunch with Lily and Levi the chocolate spot lions. It had been another good day in Crickleberry Town and Mudroot had enjoyed telling Lily all about his magic pickle stick.

THE END

Mudroot Pickles & The Big Birthday

By

Caroline George

Mudroot Pickles is the big cheese in Crickleberry town and today he needs to plan a big birthday surprise. The only problem is that the big birthday surprise is for Brian the silver pocket watch. Brian is always with Mudroot, shouting out the time and Brian doesn't like surprises.

*

'Ickle fickle, what a pickle.' Mudroot muttered as he started to dress himself. 'I think it should be stripes today.' He looked inside his wardrobe and pulled out a pair of striped socks, all different coloured stripes and a matching bow tie.

As the big cheese in Crickleberry Town, Mudroot Pickles always likes to look his best. He frowned as he spotted the glittery bow tie that he kept for special occasions. Really it should be glittery socks and tie for a big birthday but if he put on anything with glitter, then Brian would be suspicious. This was supposed to be a surprise. Brian shouted out.

ITS EIGHT O CLOCK MUDROOT!

Brian makes him jump. Mudroot dropped his bow tie and fell backwards onto his fat bottom. He let out a loud fart.

TURRUMMP!

'Oops!' Mudroot picked himself up and dusted down his clothes wondering where on earth that silly noise came from. It certainly wasn't from him.

*

Mudroot waddled through his hut to the kitchen to make himself a plate of toast and some dandelion tea. Brian would be asleep again for another hour and he had plans to make.

Friday and there's plans to make
Bright balloons and birthday cake
Brian needs some presents wrapped
Before he wakes up from his nap.

*

Mudroot combed his hair into position, his springy purple Mohican style held in place with just the right amount of raspberry jam.

*

There is a knock at the door just as Brian, the silver pocket watch, shouted out the time.

ITS NINE O CLOCK MUDROOT!

Brian made Mudroot jump again. He fell backwards onto his fat bottom and let out a loud fart.

TURRUMMP!

'Oops!' Mudroot picked himself up and dusted down his clothes, wondering where on earth that silly noise came from. It certainly wasn't from him. Nine o clock already. The day was already getting away from him.

*

Mudroot walked to his door and pulled it open. It was Mara messy monkey and Sebastian the yellow elephant who have come to help Mudroot with his plans for Brian's big birthday surprise.

'Come on in.' Mudroot smiled, his comb still stuck in his hair. 'Brian will be asleep for another fifty five minutes.' He whispered. 'As long as you don't ask him the time.' Mudroot gently eased his waistcoat off his body and passed it over to Mara messy monkey with a sleeping Brian tucked inside. 'Be very careful with this. Do not lose my waistcoat or Brian.' Mudroot watched as Mara put the waistcoat on.

'It's a bit on the large side.' She looked at Mudroot.

'Ickle, fickle, what a pickle. Then do up all of the buttons, gently. Don't wake Brian.'

'Do I have to stay here all day or can I go out?' Mara asked. 'Buddy said we could go and play by the lollipop tree today.'

'Not today. You need to stay here with Brian. We don't want him to suspect anything is wrong.'

'Boring.' Mara scowled.

'If you want to enjoy a big birthday later, someone has to do the boring stuff.' Mudroot replied.

*

Mudroot reached up to his coat stand and pulled down his long red coat. He put it on and checked his hair in the mirror, combing his Mohican back into place.

'There' he smiled, very pleased he did not leave his house this time with his comb stuck in his hair. He looked at Sebastian. 'Let's go and find some birthday presents.'

'Don't forget your pickle stick Mudroot!' Sebastian looked at him.

*

Mudroot and Sebastian walked through Crickleberry town towards the shops and stopped outside the ice cream cart.

'Good morning Gwendoline.' Mudroot smiled.

This ice cream is free and you don't have to pay
One smile and a rhyme and you're on your way.

She sang her rhyme very slowly with a low, deep voice.

'I'm very sorry Gwendoline, we don't have time to stop for ice cream today. We are off into town to buy Brian a birthday present. How are you getting on with Brian's birthday cake?'

'Baked to perfection.' She smiled. 'I took it out of the oven myself two hours ago. All I have to do is put the icing and candles on it.'

'Don't forget, will you?'

'Of course I won't forget. Buddy is coming to remind me after the table is set up.'

*

Mudroot and Sebastian walked on towards Buddy blue bear who was practicing his banjo ready to play a happy birthday song.

Happy birthday to you

This song is now due

Happy birthday grumpy Brian

Happy birthday to you

'Hello Mudroot. Hello Sebastian.' Buddy smiled. 'Do you like my song?

'It's very good.' Sebastian smiled back.

'Maybe you should change grumpy to lovely. It is his birthday after all.' Mudroot looked at him. Buddy smiled and nodded his head. 'Okay. I was going to sing it as a joke.'

Sebastian chuckled. 'Brian doesn't have a sense of humour Buddy.'

Buddy looked at Mudroot. 'Where is grumpy Brian?'

'Mara is looking after him. Brian is in my waistcoat pocket.' He stopped. 'Don't forget to remind Gwendoline about the icing for Brian's big birthday cake.'

*

Mudroot turned away and headed further along into town to Frankie's fixtures and fittings with Sebastian. The shop was closed.

'Closed for lunch?' Mudroot frowned at Sebastian. 'Frankie's never closes for lunch.' He leaned on his pickle stick. 'Ickle fickle what a pickle. We will have to wait.' Mudroot muttered, tapping his magic pickle stick on the ground. 'Come on pickle stick, a little help here please.'

*

Back at Mudroot's hut, Mara messy monkey was really, really bored and hungry. Brian the silver pocket watch stretched his arms and shouted out.

IT'S ONE O CLOCK MUDROOT!

One o clock is lunchtime for Mara. Mudroot and Sebastian were supposed to be back by now. Mara jumped down from the chair and opened the front door of Mudroot's hut. She could call in at the lollipop tree to choose a raspberry flavoured treat to keep her hunger at bay until the big birthday party.

*

Mara walked on, past the icky sticky bun bush, towards Talia tiger who was putting some colourful polish on her claws.

'Hello Mara. Are you all ready for the big birthday party?'

'Yes but I'm really hungry so I am going over to the lollipop tree to get something to eat.'

'I thought you were looking after Brian?' Talia looked at her.

'I am.' Mara pointed down to the waistcoat pocket. 'He's asleep.'

'Where?' Talia asked as she peered down inside the pocket. 'Brian isn't in there.'

Mara gasped and put her hand up to her mouth. She pulled open the pocket and looked inside. There was no Brian.

'Oh no! I must have lost him. Mudroot will be very cross.'

'Don't worry Mara, we can look for him together. Jump up on my back and we will go and ask the others where he is.'

*

Talia padded down the lane towards the lemonade fountain where Buddy blue bear was still practicing his song.

Happy birthday to you

This song is now due

Happy birthday lovely Brian

Happy birthday to you

'Hello Talia. Hello Mara. Do you like my big birthday song?' Buddy asked.

'It's very good.' Talia said. 'Have you seen Brian anywhere?'

Buddy looked at Mara. 'I thought you were looking after Brian.'

'I lost him. Mudroot will be very cross with me.' Mara looked at Buddy.

'Then I'll help you to find him. Brian can't have gone very far.'

*

The three friends stopped off at the lollipop tree for a quick snack. Sybil swirly snake was trying on some party hats.

'Hello Talia. Hello Mara. Hello Buddy. Where are you all going?'

'We are trying to find Brian the silver pocket watch.' Mara said. 'Have you seen him?'

Before Sybil could answer, Oscar, the one eyed owl, swooped down, holding an envelope in his beak.

'I have another birthday card for Brian.' He landed on a branch and dropped the green envelope down onto the grass.

'I will add it to the pile on the table.' Buddy smiled. Then he stopped. Then he looked at his friends. 'Oh no!' He said.

'What's wrong Buddy?' The friends chorused.

'What time is it?'

The friends looked from one to the other, shaking their heads.

'Without Brian to shout at us we don't know what time it is?' They said.

'I was supposed to remind Gwendoline to ice the birthday cake. I was so busy with my song I forgot.' He hung his head down. 'Mudroot will be very cross with me too.'

'Let's go and find Gwendoline and remind her about the birthday cake. Then we will go and look for Brian.'

*

Gwendoline giraffe was ironing her glittery purple party dress when the friends approached.

'Hello Talia. Hello Mara. Hello Buddy. Hello Sybil. Hello Oscar. Do you like my party dress?' She held it up for them to see.

'It's very nice.' Mara said.

'Where are you off to? The party isn't until two o clock.'

'Have you iced Brian's big birthday cake?' Buddy looked at her.

Gwendoline shook her head. 'No. Not yet. Is it time?'

'We don't know what time it is. Brian has gone missing.' Mara looked at Gwendoline.

'Missing?'

'We will find him.' Talia said.

*

'Can you ice the big birthday cake and put it on the table?' Buddy looked at Gwendoline.

'Not without some help. It's a very big cake.' Just then Levi and Lily the chocolate spot lion's appear.

'The table is ready. We have lemonade, icky sticky buns, orange jelly and fruity lollipops. All we need now is the big birthday cake.' Levi looked at Gwendoline.

'I forgot to ice it. I was ironing my party dress.' Gwendoline said.

'And I forgot to remind her because I was practicing my song.' Buddy said.

'And I wasn't able to keep an eye on the time because I've lost Brian the silver pocket watch.' Mara said.

'Where is Mudroot Pickles?' Lily asked.

'Shopping for a birthday present with Sebastian. He was supposed to be back ages ago.' Mara said.

'It's a right old mess we've got ourselves into.' Levi scratched his head.

Just then, Oscar flew above them. 'He's coming back. I can see him?'

'Who? Brian?' Mara asked.

'No. Mudroot and Sebastian. Looks like they have lots of presents.'

*

Mudroot smiled one of his big megawatt smiles.

'Looks like you are all ready for the big birthday party.' He watched as all of the animals looked down at the floor.

'What's wrong?' He set down his bags.

'I forgot to ice the cake. I was ironing my party dress.' Gwendoline said.

'And I forgot to remind her because I was practicing my song.' Buddy said.

'And I wasn't able to keep an eye on the time because I've lost Brian the silver pocket watch.' Mara hung her head.

'Ickle, fickle, what a pickle.' Mudroot scratched his head.

*

Mudroot has the biggest, kindest heart in the world and he doesn't like telling anyone off but he felt very disappointed. He frowned.

'Then how are we going to fix this?'

'We have to ice the cake.' Gwendoline said.

'We have to find Brian.' Mara said.

Mudroot looked at his friends. ‘Gwendoline and Buddy can ice the cake and Levi and Lily can carry it to the table. Oscar, can you put the candles on the top please?’ He turned to the others. ‘We will go and look for Brian.’ He adjusted his glasses and looked at Mara. ‘Where were you when you last saw Brian?’

‘At the hut. I only left when Brian told me it was one o clock. I was hungry.’

‘You and your grumbling belly are forever getting you into trouble.’ Mudroot tapped his pickle stick on the ground. ‘Come on pickle stick where should we start looking? The lemonade fountain?’

The pickle stick did not move.

‘The icky sticky bun bush?’

The pickle stick did not move.

'The candy floss fence?'

The pickle stick did not move.

'My hut?' Mudroot asked and the pickle stick started to wobble. 'To the hut. Brian must be somewhere close by.

*

Mudroot and his friends made their way back to Mudroot's hut to see if they could find Brian.

'He's very small Mudroot. He will be hard to spot.' Talia said.

'If we can get close to where he is, I can ask him the time. Brian will answer. He might be pretty grumpy about it, but he will answer.' Mudroot opened the front door of his hut.

'What time is it please Brian?'

*

All eyes were on the hut, the garden outside, the table and chairs inside. Out of the corner of his eye Mudroot saw a pair of silver arms stretch out next to the purple velvet cushion. Brian yawned and stretched, feeling a little bad tempered that he had been disturbed before the hour. He shouted.

ITS ONLY TEN MINUTES TO TWO MUDROOT!

There is a moment of silence before Brian continued.

WHO LEFT ME ON THE FLOOR THIS MORNING IN AMONGST THE DIRT AND THE SPIDERS? JUST LEFT ME THERE TO FIND MY OWN WAY BACK TO A COSY SPOT?

'Brian.' They all chorused. 'We missed you.' Mudroot scooped Brian up from the cushion and tucked him back inside his now glittery waistcoat. Brian shouted out.

GLITTER? NOT ANOTHER BIG PARADE MUDROOT?

'Not a parade but I hear that someone has a very special day today. A big birthday.' He smiled as Brian's cheeks flushed pink. 'Come on Brian, let's go. We don't want to be late.'

*

Over at the birthday table the friends were struggling to light the candles on the birthday cake. Even Gwendoline, who was tall enough to reach up couldn't do it.

'I can't light the candles on the birthday cake.' Gwendoline said.

'Ickle fickle what a pickle. Mudroot held up his pickle stick and started to chant.

A little bit of magic

A tiny flick and click

A few quick sparks

With my magic pickle stick.

All the animals stared, as each spark from the pickle stick lit the candles.

'Magic!' Gwendoline said. 'Now it looks like a big birthday cake.

*

As the clock struck two the animals gathered at the back of the curious cabbage patch to celebrate Brian's birthday. Gwendoline wore her best dress with purple glitter. Talia showed off her painted claws. Oscar, the one eyed owl, made sure all of the candles stayed on top of the big birthday cake that was oozing with strawberry icing.

Swirly Sybil snake made sure everyone had a party hat. Mara made sure Brian stayed safe inside Mudroot's waistcoat pocket, even when Mudroot jumped with another bottom trumpet.

Levi and Lily lion made sure the table was full of delicious food; icky sticky buns, jellies that wobbled on plates and lollipops in a hundred different flavours. There was plenty of lemonade in jugs and lemonade sweets for everyone. There was singing from Buddy blue bear and lots of dancing from the harlequin hedgehogs as Brian blew out all of his candles.

Happy birthday to you

This song is now due

Happy birthday lovely Brian

Happy birthday to you

*

With Brian full of cake and tucked up for the night Mudroot pulled on his purple silk Pyjamas and switched off the light. It had been another busy day but a wonderful big birthday.

THE END

Mudroot Pickles' Big Easter Egg Hunt

by

Caroline George

As Mudroot sat down in his favourite armchair with a plate of toast, dripping with dollops of gooseberry jelly, he looked at the two easter eggs sitting on his bookcase. One was his easter treat, picked up from the all in one shop and ready to eat on Easter Sunday. The other egg was twice the size of his friend Evie's head and displayed in a wicker basket. It was a milk chocolate egg tied around the middle with a yellow ribbon. In the bottom of the basket sat lots of small chocolate eggs. This egg was not for Mudroot Pickles. This egg was the first prize for the winner of the easter egg hunt. Mudroot smiled to himself. It was going to be a busy day.

‘What time is it Brian?’ Mudroot’s voice boomed down to Brian the silver pocket watch. Brian yawned, feeling a little bad tempered he had been disturbed before the hour. He shouted out.

WHAT DO YOU WANT MUDROOT? ITS ONLY A QUARTER TO NINE!

Time for Frankie to visit with the supply of eggs for the easter egg hunt thought Mudroot, popping the last bite of toast into his mouth and savouring the last lick of gooseberry jelly. He stood up and took his empty plate over to the sink, dropping it down into the soapy water. The plate could stay in the suds until the end of the day. At six o clock Brian would shout at him to remember to wash it up before he went to bed.

*

There was a knock at the door. ‘Morning Mudroot.’ Came the familiar voice of Frankie from Frankie’s fixtures and fittings. Frankie could get his hands on anything, including a good supply of easter eggs.

‘Come on in Frankie, the door is open.’ Mudroot called.

‘Here you go. One box of foil wrapped chocolate eggs. And three dozen eggs to paint and a box of paints.’ He grinned. ‘What time does the hunt start tomorrow?’

‘Ten o clock. We’ll all be helping to paint the eggs today and then I will be hiding them around the woodland later tonight.’ Mudroot smiled.

'So that's why you have that old table set up in your garden.' Frankie replied.

*

Mudroot had set up the old wallpaper table to give him and his friends plenty of room to paint eggs. He peered inside the box of paints, delighted to see paints of all different colours. There were three different shades of yellow, lovely purples, rich reds, even some silver and gold paint. Mudroot felt very pleased.

'Thank you Frankie. This all looks great.' He smiled one of his best smiles.

Mudroot was setting out the paints and brushes on the table when Levi and Lily the chocolate spot lion's arrived to help paint some easter eggs. Mudroot passed Levi a couple of empty jam jars.

'Can you fill them up with water and put the brushes in them.'

'You are very well organised today Mudroot.' Lily smiled as Gwendoline parked her ice cream cart outside Mudroot's hut.

This ice cream is free and you don't have to pay
One smile and a rhyme and you're on your way.

Gwendoline sang her rhyme very slowly with her low, deep voice. Lily decided that she would quite like an ice cream this early in the day.

I love ice cream, vanilla's the best
If I drop it, the colour won't ruin my vest

Gwendoline scooped out one splodge of vanilla ice cream and passed it to Lily as Buddy blue bear arrived to help.

ice cream for breakfast is a special treat
two scoops please while I take my seat

Buddy blue bear smiled and sat down at the table with a double cornet of mint chocolate chip and banana.

*

Mudroot clapped his hands once all the friends were sat down around the table. He wanted to make sure that everyone painted at least two eggs. There were no rules to follow. His friends just had to make the eggs look as colourful as possible.

Mudroot sat down at the head of the table and picked up his first egg.

CRACK. SMASH. CRACK!

Oh dear! The egg shell shattered and Mudroot's hands, shirt sleeves and the table were covered in egg yolk and goo. Mudroot cried out in astonishment as his friends all had the same problem. In seconds the table was covered in slimy, messy, sticky, eggy goo.

'Ickle fickle what a pickle.' Mudroot stood up as the egg yolks started to run down the table and off the edge. He stepped back and slipped on the egg yolk, falling down onto his fat bottom with a big fart.

TURRUMMP!

'Oops!' Mudroot picked himself up and dusted down his clothes, wondering where on earth that silly noise came from. It certainly wasn't from him.

He watched as Buddy reached for another egg.

'Stop!' Mudroot boomed so loud he made Buddy jump so high that he dropped another egg.

CRACK. SMASH. CRACK!

'FRANKIE!' Mudroot roared, realising that Frankie had forgotten to hard boil the eggs before delivering them to be painted. There was eggy mess everywhere.

The yellow yolk was stuck in Levi's mane making his fur stand out in stupid places. It was all caught up in Buddy's paws making everything stick to them; paint brushes, pens and eggshell. Yolks ran down Gwendoline's legs, pooling underneath her feet, making her lose her balance, just like Mudroot. Gwendoline wobbled, she swayed, she stumbled around as her legs gave way underneath and then she fell over onto her back, her four legs in the air. The sticky goo tickled the end of Sebastian's trunk and made him sneeze. The massive sneeze blew more eggy goo over the other animals and left the whole table in a right sticky mess.

'Ickle fickle what a pickle.' Said Mudroot. 'This is turning out to be a disastrous day.'

*

Evie pulled up outside Mudroot's hut on her scooter.

'Are you making an omelet?' She asked.

'No Evie. We are making a mess.' Talia tiger smiled.

'Buddy said that you are painting eggs today.' Evie looked at the broken shells all over the table. 'You can't paint broken shells.' She laughed. Mudroot turned raspberry red. He had done everything right with all the eggs, all the paints and all the colours. Trust Frankie to make such a stupid mistake.

'We need to cook the eggs first.' Mudroot said, lifting up the box of eggs. He looked at Evie. 'Why don't you help clean up the mess and I will go and boil these eggs so that you all have something to paint.'

Evie looked across to Gwendoline's ice cream cart hopefully.

'Ice cream after a good clean up.' Mudroot walked inside his hut.

*

As Mudroot watched the eggs boil inside the largest pan he owned, Sebastian the yellow elephant took charge of the clean-up. He was more than happy to help with soapy suds and water for the table, but first the animals had to forget about their sticky paws and clear the table.

Oscar, the one eyed owl, swooped down to pick up broken egg shells, passing these over to Lily and Levi, the chocolate spot lions, to put in a bin. Buddy blue bear and Mara messy monkey carry the box of paints and pens away from the mucky table and set it down on the grass next to Mudroot's motorbike. Talia tiger and Gwendoline put the paint brushes and pencils back inside jam jars. The harlequin hedgehogs start to clear away beakers of juice. Once the table is clear of mess, Evie holds a bucket of soapy water and Sebastian hoses away the eggy mess with his trunk.

'All done.' Evie laughed, looking at Gwendoline who walked slowly over to her ice cream cart.

This ice cream is free and you don't have to pay

One rhyme and a smile and you're on your way

Gwendoline opened up the lid of her cart, allowing a waft of sugary ice cream to fill the air.

At the ice cream cart I'm first in line

A toffee sludge will be just fine

Evie chuckled and watched as Gwendoline plopped a scoop of brown ice cream on top of a cornet.

*

Mudroot appeared outside his front door with a triumphant look on his face.

'All done. Who is ready to paint?' He smiled, stepping down the wooden steps towards the table. As he stepped past his motorbike, he did not see the box of paints sticking out from the side. One minute he was walking proudly with a box of eggs ready to be painted, the next, he falls over.

All the animal's gasped and covered their eyes.

'Oh no. Please don't fall Mudroot. We've only just cleaned up this mess.'

As the box flies up in the air and the eggs leap out of the box, Oscar, the one eyed owl, caught two eggs in his wings. Buddy dived forward to catch another two in his paws. Mara lassoed two in her tail and Sybil curled her body around into a pot shape to provide a soft landing for three eggs. But, lots of eggs landed on the path along with Mudroot who landed with a thud on his bottom, letting out a loud fart.

TURRUMMP!

'Oops!' Mudroot picked himself up and dusted down his clothes, wondering where on earth that silly noise came from. It certainly wasn't from him.

Evie chuckled. 'My mummy says that you have to say excuse me when you trump like that.'

'Why are you looking at me.' Mudroot was all red in the face.

'You trumped.' The little girl laughed.

'I did not!' Mudroot dusted himself off and looked at the eggs.

Lily and Levi lions had their paws over their eyes, afraid to look. Sebastian wandered off to get some more water and soap, already thinking about the next clean up.

Mudroot laughed. 'It's alright. The eggs are cooked. They didn't break this time.'

Slowly, Levi and Lily moved their paws away from their eyes to see that Mudroot was telling the truth. There was no eggy mess anywhere, just lots of unpainted eggs on the gravel and on the grass.

'Shall we get back to some painting.' Mudroot said.

*

The hours flew by with the friends busy painting the small eggs in lots of different colours. There were stripes and spots on some, curly swirly lines on others. Gwendoline had made use of the gold and silver paint and one of the eggs she painted was midnight blue with lots of stars on it. Slowly but surely the box of ordinary hard boiled eggs was replaced with a box full of brightly coloured easter treasure, every bit as colourful as a box of Christmas decorations.

Brian the silver pocket watch stretched out his arms and shouted out.

ITS FOUR O CLOCK MUDROOT!

Brian made Mudroot jump but this time, because Mudroot was sitting down at the table with his friends, he barely moved. He noticed that Brian did not fold himself back inside his waistcoat pocket.

'Brian. Do you need something?' Mudroot asked.

YOU SAID THERE WOULD BE OATMEAL AND BLACKBERRY COOKIES AT FOUR O CLOCK. WHERE ARE THEY? I COULD DO WITH A SNACK.

Brian shouted, feeling very grumpy and very hungry. Mudroot shuffled off the bench with a chuckle.

'Yes I did didn't I. They're on a plate on the kitchen table. I'll go and get them. We could all do with a snack.'

With all the cookies demolished and all the eggs painted and dry, the friends made their way back to their own houses. Everyone needed to get a good night's sleep ahead of the easter egg hunt.

*

The sun was shining brightly when Mudroot woke up. He had a later night than his friends because he was the one responsible for hiding all the easter eggs. It had taken him hours, loading up the mini chocolate eggs and the painted eggs into the sidecar of his motorbike and then scattering them through the woodland.

He looked again at the first prize easter egg wrapped up in a basket and then at his own chocolate easter egg that he planned to share with Brian later. As he finished his dandelion tea he could hear the excited chatter of the group gathering outside.

Inside his waistcoat pocket Brian stretched and yawned. He shouted out.

ITS NINE O CLOCK MUDROOT. TIME FOR THE EASTER EGG HUNT!

Mudroot pulled on his long velvet coat and walked towards his front door.

'Who's ready for an easter egg hunt?' He boomed as he opened his front door and stood on the threshold.

Mudroot looked around at his friends. All of them had remembered to bring something to carry their eggs in. Buddy had his bobble hat. Gwendoline had her orange handbag. The harlequin hedgehogs carry a box between them. Levi and Lily are wearing crochet bags around their necks. Mara and Talia are using old saucepans and Sebastian had his yellow bucket.

'Wait.' Mudroot stopped and disappeared inside his hut. A minute later he returned with the first prize chocolate egg. The friends gasped. The egg was massive. 'This is for the winner. For the person who collects the most eggs.' He smiled as Evie arrived on her bicycle with a small basket. She hopped off, very excited to be joining the animals easter egg hunt.

Mudroot stood at the top of his steps giving out instructions. The hunt will last for one hour. Mudroot and Frankie will count the eggs. The winner will be announced at eleven o clock by Brian the silver pocket watch.

'Off you go.' Mudroot clapped his hands and watched as the friends rushed off in different directions.

Can you see any easter eggs in the long grass?

Mara monkey spotted what looked like a blue foil wrapper sticking out past the licorice lamp post and raced towards it. Her first easter egg. She raced on.

Can you see any easter eggs down by the apple trees?

Sebastian the yellow elephant spotted what looked like yellow and red spots peeping out from the side of the tree trunk and ambled towards it. He remembered Levi the chocolate spot lion painting a yellow and red egg. He picked it up with his trunk. It was his fourth easter egg.

Can you see any easter eggs by the icky sticky bun bushes?

Levi spotted what looked like a rainbow striped egg and leapt towards it. He picked it up with his paw and dropped it inside his crochet bag with three others.

Can you see any easter eggs by the lollipop tree?

Buddy blue bear spotted the pink foil wrapper as the sun glittered across it and jumped over the grass to pick it up. His fifth egg of the day. Maybe this would be enough for the first prize. Buddy carried on searching.

*

In the distance Mudroot heard the excited cries, that one of his friends had found an egg, start to die down. This was a sign that all the eggs had probably been found. He reached for his whistle and blew into it as hard as he could to signal the end of the easter egg hunt.

'Time's up! Bring your eggs to the hut and Frankie and I will do a count.'

The friends dropped off their easter egg haul and gathered around Gwendoline's ice cream cart for a much needed treat. Mudroot and Frankie disappeared inside the hut to count the easter eggs.

Mudroot scratched his head and looked at Frankie.

'Ickle fickle what a pickle. Everyone has found the same number of eggs.' He scratched his head. 'We will have to count them all again.'

Frankie looked at Mudroot. 'They have all collected six eggs each.'

'Oh dear.' Mudroot looked at Frankie. 'We only have one first prize.' He stood up and started to pace the floor.

Brian stretched out his hands and blinked.

ITS ELEVEN O CLOCK MUDROOT, WHO IS THE WINNER?

'Ickle fickle what a pickle. We don't have one winner Brian, we have too many. Everyone found six eggs. What are we going to do?'

TOSS A COIN UNTIL YOU GET A WINNER.

Brian shouted out.

'Do an easter quiz to get the winner instead.' Said Frankie.

Mudroot shook his head and reached for his pickle stick.

'No. We can't keep doing quizzes or playing more games until we get a winner. My friends want to enjoy their easter eggs.' He twirled his pickle stick around. 'I have an idea.' He smiled, whispering to Brian what to announce.

AND THE WINNER OF TODAY'S EASTER EGG HUNT IS.

Brian stopped deliberately as Mudroot held the large first prize egg in his hands. Brian smiled as all of the friends held their breath.

EVERYONE! YOU ALL COLLECTED SIX EGGS!

'But there is only one first prize. We can't all win.' Sybil hissed to a muttered chorus of agreement.

'You each have six eggs in your baskets, plenty already to enjoy. With my magic pickle stick I can make the first prize go a little further than an egg for one.' Mudroot lifted up his pickle stick and struck the top of the egg with a tap or two.

A little bit of magic

A tiny tap and click

A few quick knocks

With my magic pickle stick.

The friends gasped as the easter egg broke into lots of pieces.

'There is plenty here for everyone.' Mudroot smiled as the friends stepped forward to take a piece of chocolate.

*

With all the eggs eaten and the easter egg hunt a big success, Mudroot pulled on his purple silk Pyjamas and switched off his light. It had been another busy day at Crickleberry Town and a wonderful easter egg hunt.

THE END

Mudroot Pickles' Big Parade

By

Caroline George

Mudroot Pickles is the big cheese in Crickleberry town. He has a booming voice that is loud enough to make the trees shake. Mudroot is only as tall as a rugby ball but what he lacks in height, he makes up for with his big smiley, super white false teeth; a smile from Frankie's fixtures and fittings that dazzle the other animals.

*

As the big cheese in Crickleberry, Mudroot Pickles is the best dressed hedgehog in town. He wears a bright white shirt with a bow tie and a pair of striped trousers held up with a gold tasseled string. Mudroot loves his bow ties; tartan, striped, spots, and he has a glittery bow tie for special occasions, like today.

*

Mudroot has matching socks, big and sloppy, that wrinkled over his hairy ankles and because Mudroot is a very important hedgehog, he wears thick rimmed spectacles and has a checked waistcoat where he keeps Brian, his silver pocket watch. Brian shouts out the time to Mudroot whenever the clock strikes the hour. Sometimes, Brian can be grumpy, especially if Mudroot disturbs him to ask for the time. Grumpy old Brian!

*

To keep him warm Mudroot wears a long velvet coat. He has lots of different colours, including purple to match his Mohican style haircut. To keep him well fed Mudroot helps himself to any number of Crickleberry town delights. He might stop off by the icky sticky bun bush for an iced bun and once a week he will invite himself over to Frankie's for a vegetable stew with lots of dumplings.

*

To keep him out of trouble, which is the most important thing of all, Mudroot has a magic pickle stick. A magic pickle stick is a very important stick to have. It can find anything that is lost. It can help fix cuts and bruises. It can even give Mudroot Pickles a good clue about what to do next. As long as Mudroot remembers his magic pickle stick he will always stay out of trouble.

*

Brian the silver pocket watch shouts out.

IT'S TWELVE O CLOCK MUDROOT!

Brian makes him jump. Mudroot falls backwards onto his fat bottom and lets out a loud fart.

TURRUMMP!

'Oops!' Mudroot picked himself up and dusted down his clothes, wondering where on earth that silly noise came from. It certainly wasn't from him.

*

Today is very important because Mudroot and his friends are getting ready for the big parade.

Tuesday and there's lots to do

Mudroot is meeting his pickle crew

He'll be there to join the queue

Precisely when the clock strikes two

*

Mudroot was combing his hair into position, a springy purple Mohican style that needed just the right amount of raspberry jam to hold it into place. There was a knock at the door just as Brian, the silver pocket watch, shouted out the time.

ITS ONE O CLOCK MUDROOT! HAVE YOU HAD YOUR LUNCH?

Brian makes Mudroot jump again. He falls backwards onto his fat bottom and lets out a loud fart.

TURRUMMP!

'Oops!' Mudroot picked himself up and dusted down his clothes, wondering where on earth that silly noise came from. It certainly wasn't from him.

*

Someone was early for the big parade. Mudroot walked to his door and pulled it open. It was Levi the chocolate spot lion and something was wrong. Levi was covered in a blanket which was not like him at all.

'You're early.' Mudroot frowned, his comb still stuck in his hair.

'I have a problem.' Levi's cheeks flushed pink and he looked very embarrassed. 'Look! My chocolate spots, they've all gone.' Levi pulled his blanket up. Mudroot adjusted his spectacles. The chocolate spots were all gone.

'Ickle, fickle, what a pickle. We will have to find them before the big parade.' Mudroot said.

*

Mudroot reached up to his coat stand and pulled down his long coat. He put it on and checked his hair in the mirror, combing his Mohican back into place.

'There' he smiled, very pleased he did not leave his house with his comb stuck in his hair. 'Come on Levi. Let's go and find your chocolate spots.'

'Don't forget your pickle stick Mudroot!' Levi looked at him.

*

Mudroot and Levi walked through Crickleberry town. They stopped outside the house where Sebastian the yellow elephant lived. Sebastian was the chief animal washer and he makes sure everyone has a wash.

Watch out for his sponges! They tickle and make you giggle.

Sebastian was polishing his trumpet for the big parade.

'Hello Mudroot. Hello Levi.' He smiled, his voice high pitched and squeaky. Then Sebastian frowned. 'Why are you covered up in a blanket Levi?'

'Have you seen Levi's chocolate spots?' Mudroot asked.

Sebastian shook his big yellow head. 'No.'

Levi lowered his head. 'I can't join the big parade without my chocolate spots.'

'I will keep my eyes open and sound my trumpet, like this, if I find them.' Sebastian blows into his trumpet.

BUPP BUPP BURRUPP

'Thank you, Sebastian. We will keep looking. See you at the parade at two o clock.' Mudroot said.

*

Mudroot and Levi walked on towards Buddy blue bear who looked after the lemonade fountain. Buddy was practicing his banjo ready for the big parade.

'Hello Mudroot. Hello Levi.' Buddy smiled. 'Why are you covered up in a blanket Levi?'

'Have you seen Levi's chocolate spots?' Mudroot asked.

Buddy shook his head. ‘No.’

Levi lowered his head. ‘I can’t join the big parade without my chocolate spots.’

‘I will keep my eyes open and play my banjo extra loud, like this, if I find them.’

PURUMM, STURUMM, TURWANNG!

Buddy looked at Mudroot. ‘I have a problem too.’ He pointed to the lemonade fountain. ‘Someone has drunk all the lemonade. The fountain is almost dry. I have some lemonade sweets but I can’t join the big parade without bottles of lemonade.’

‘Ickle fickle what a pickle. We will have to find some more lemonade too,’ muttered Mudroot, tapping his magic pickle stick on the ground. 'Come on pickle stick, a little help here please.' He said.

*

Mudroot and Levi walked on, past the icky sticky bun bush, towards Talia tiger. Talia was practicing with her maracas ready for the big parade.

Double shake up

Double shake down

Shake those maracas

Through Crickleberry town

She chanted, as she rattled her maracas. 'Oh, hello Mudroot. Hello Levi.' Talia smiled. 'Why are you covered up in a blanket Levi?'

'Have you seen Levi's chocolate spots?' Mudroot asked.

Talia shook her head. 'No.'

Levi lowered his head. 'I can't join the big parade without my chocolate spots.'

Mudroot looked at Talia again. 'Do you know anything about Buddy's lemonade fountain? Someone has drunk it dry.'

Talia shook her head again. 'No, sorry. I haven't seen any chocolate spots or lemonade. But I will keep my eyes open and do a double shake in the air of my maracas, like this, if I find them.'

SHAKE, RATTLE, SHAKE!

'Ickle, fickle what a pickle. Missing chocolate spots and missing lemonade' muttered Mudroot, tapping his magic pickle stick on the ground. 'Come on pickle stick, time to wake up and point me in the right direction.' He tutted.

*

As they walked past the harlequin hedgehogs who were practicing their song and dance for the big parade, a very green, messy Mara monkey walked towards Mudroot and Levi holding onto her belly.

'My tummy hurts. I can't play the triangle for the big parade. I need some magic medicine.' She groaned.

'**You!**' Mudroot pointed his pickle stick at Mara. 'You have eaten all of Levi's chocolate spots and drunk all the lemonade.'

'No, it wasn't me?' Mara said.

‘That’s why you have a tummy ache. Too much chocolate and too much lemonade. You are a very naughty monkey.’ Mudroot scolded.

‘No, it wasn’t me!’ Mara let out a big burp.

BBURRPP!

‘Proof!’ Mudroot laughed. ‘If you drink too much lemonade it makes you burp.’

‘It wasn’t me!’ Mara groaned, still holding her belly.

*

Mudroot has the biggest, kindest heart in the world and he doesn’t like telling anyone off, but Mara was a very naughty monkey who was always hungry and was always very greedy.

Mudroot frowned. ‘I am very cross with you Mara.’

*

Just then Mudroot heard Gwendoline giraffe, who looked after the ice cream cart. Gwendoline was stood at the end of the street, by the red clock tower.

This ice cream is free and you don't have to pay

One smile and a rhyme and you're on your way.

She sang her rhyme very slowly with a low, deep voice. Mudroot's pickle stick started to wobble.

'Finally.' Mudroot smiled. 'A sign.' Mudroot listened as he heard another rhyme and then a giggle but this time the voice did not belong to Gwendoline. This voice was high and squeaky, like it came from a little person.

Here I am at the ice cream cart

Raspberry ripple makes me fart.

The voice giggled and as Mudroot raced towards the ice cream cart he spotted a little boy with brown curls taking an ice cream from Gwendoline.

*

Mudroot looked up and spotted Oscar, the one-eyed owl, swooping down to take a large beak full of the rippled cornet, before the little boy took one lick. The boy shrieked and ran towards the lollipop tree.

'Give that back you naughty owl.'

As the little boy looked up, Mudroot was just in time to see him being scooped up by Sybil swirly snake into the lollipop tree. There was another shriek from the little boy who was now hanging upside down.

'Put me down you naughty snake or I'll tell my Mummy!'

All the animals gasped in horror, looking at Mudroot. 'She can't tell her mummy, we'll all get into trouble!'

*

Mudroot pulled Brian, the silver pocket watch, out of his pocket to check the time. Brian yawned, feeling a little bad tempered he had been disturbed before the hour. He shouted.

WHAT DO YOU WANT MUDROOT? ITS ONLY A QUARTER TO TWO. SOME OF US NEED OUR BEAUTY SLEEP!

*

'Ickle, fickle what a pickle. Missing chocolate spots, missing lemonade, Mara's bellyache and now a little boy who is too early for the big parade.' Mudroot tapped his pickle stick that seemed to be no help today.

He tipped his glasses towards Sybil, about to say something, when his shoes slid onto the slippery ice cream. He fell backwards, onto his fat bottom which let out the loudest fart anyone had ever heard.

'Oops!' Mudroot said as another fart blasted out. Where was that noise coming from? It certainly wasn't from him.

*

The upside-down little boy laughed. 'My Mummy calls them bottom trumpets.' He giggled as Mudroot scrambled to his feet looking most put out.

'They are not bottom trumpets young man. They are fluff puffs.' He stared at Sybil. 'Come on now Sybil, what have we said about your hugs!'

'Only for those who want them.' She fluttered her eye lashes at Mudroot and gave a quick shake of her tambourine.

JANGLE, JINGLE, JANGLE!

Mudroot looked at the little boy. 'And who are you?'

'I'm Milo. That owl ate my ice cream and this snake won't let me go.'

'Sybil!' Mudroot frowned as Sybil uncoiled her body to let Milo drop onto the grass with a gentle plop.

Mudroot helped Milo back up onto his feet. 'The big parade is not until two o clock. You shouldn't be here.'

'Why not?'

'Because then Oscar wouldn't have eaten your ice cream and Sybil wouldn't have pulled you up into the lollipop tree and given you a hug that you didn't want.' He smiled.

'Ask him about my chocolate spots?' Levi said.

'And ask him about my lemonade.' Buddy frowned.

Mudroot adjusted his glasses. 'Did you eat Levi's chocolate spots and drink all the lemonade?'

'I didn't eat all of the chocolate spots. They are in my bag.'

'And the lemonade?' Mudroot looked at the little boy.

Milo looked down at the grass, ashamed. 'I drank it all, sorry.' His bottom lip started to wobble and he began to cry. He turned to run away but tripped over Levi's tail.

'Ickle fickle what a pickle. This is turning out to be a disastrous day.' Mudroot said.

Mudroot passed Milo his handkerchief to dry his tears and carefully inspected his knee. It was just a teeny, tiny, scratch but there was some blood.

'Oh no.' Levi looked shocked. 'Will his leg fall off?'

Mudroot laughed. 'Heavens no. It is just a teeny, tiny scratch.' He held up his pickle stick and started to chant.

A little bit of magic

A tiny tap and click

A few quick dabs

With my magic pickle stick.

All the animals stared as one dab of magical glittery cream soothed the grazed knee.

Milo stared, eyes wide. 'Magic!' He stopped crying.

'Just like magic.' Mudroot smiled as Buddy stuck the chocolate buttons back onto Levi.

'Thank you, Buddy. We have just enough time to go and pick up some more lemonade from Frankie's.'

Mudroot looped his arm around Mara. 'I'm sorry for telling you off Mara. Come back to my hut and we'll sort out some magic medicine for that sore belly before the big parade.'

*

IT'S TWO O CLOCK MUDROOT!

Shouted Brian the silver pocket watch.

As the clock struck two the whole of Crickleberry town lined the street to see Mudroot Pickles lead the procession for the big parade. There was singing and lots of dancing as the animals marched past the green and yellow fields, across the wooden bridge and down the high street that was decorated with pretty flowers.

They played their instruments as they passed the bakers shop, the fruit stalls and the all in one shop. Everyone in the town cheered and clapped and waved flags as Mudroot Pickles and his marching band played through the town.

Up front, behind Mudroot Pickles, marched messy Mara monkey proudly playing her triangle and swirly Sybil snake rattling her tambourine. Next came the dancing harlequin hedgehogs in splendid singing voices, followed by Talia tiger shaking her maracas.

Buddy blue bear followed, playing his banjo and throwing out lemonade sweets for the children. Next to Buddy, Sebastian the yellow elephant played his trumpet.

Levi lion held up the rear with his big bass drum, with enough chocolate spots to cover his coat. Oscar, the one-eyed owl, flew above, keeping a look out for any of his favourite ice creams.

Thanks to Mudroot Pickles there was enough lemonade for everyone and thanks to Gwendoline, Crickleberry Town had all the ice cream it could eat.

*

With Milo back at home and Mudroot's friends tucked up for the night, Mudroot pulled on his purple silk Pyjamas and switched off his light. It had been another busy day in Crickleberry town but a wonderful big parade.

THE END

Mudroot Pickles' Big Day Out

By

Caroline George

As the big cheese in Crickleberry Town, Mudroot Pickles likes to take charge. Today he has organised a day out at Crickleberry Park. His friends have been very excited about their trip and have all sent some yummy food to go inside the picnic basket.

*

Gwendoline giraffe will bring her ice cream cart. Buddy is bringing drinks and sweets from his lemonade fountain. Lily and Levi, the chocolate spot lions, have picked some of the green leaves that Mudroot and Sebastian really like. Mara messy monkey has a box of iced buns from the icky sticky bun bush. Sybil swirly snake has a bag filled with fruity treats from the lollipop tree. Oscar, the one-eyed owl, and Talia tiger have picked some sugary snacks from the candy floss fence. Sebastian has made some gooseberry jam and has volunteered to drive the bus to the park. The harlequin hedgehogs are bringing some strings of licorice from the licorice lamp posts. Evie has made some sausage rolls and Milo has a large bag of peanuts. With such a feast already filling the picnic hamper, all Mudroot has to bring is a large flask of dandelion tea.

*

Brian shouted out.

ITS TEN O CLOCK MUDROOT!

Brian made him jump. Mudroot falls backwards onto his fat bottom and lets out a loud fart.

TURRUMMP!

'Oops!' Mudroot picked himself up and dusted down his clothes, wondering where on earth that silly noise came from. It certainly wasn't from him.

*

Mudroot pulled back his curtain and checked the weather outside. He popped his false teeth inside his mouth and smiled his big gleaming smile. Today it was sunny and there was not one cloud in the sky.

Thursday and there's lots to do

All arranged by you know who

Picnic goodies for all to eat

At the park, so hard to beat

Mudroot checked the picnic hamper again. All the food was inside, drinks too and Frankie gave him a box of cutlery, cups and plates. Mudroot scratched his head, wondering what was missing and instantly spoiled his hair. He looked at himself in the mirror and pulled a stupid face.

'Ickle fickle what a pickle. I can't go out with my hair looking like this.' Mudroot stood in front of the mirror combing his hair back into position, a springy purple Mohican style that needed just the right amount of raspberry jam to hold it into place.

*

There was a knock at the door just as Brian, the silver pocket watch, shouted out the time.

ITS ELEVEN O CLOCK MUDROOT!

Brian made Mudroot jump again. He falls backwards onto his fat bottom and lets out a loud fart.

TURRUMMP!

'Oops!' Mudroot picked himself up and dusted down his clothes, wondering where on earth that silly noise came from. It certainly wasn't from him.

*

Mudroot opened his front door. Levi was stood on the step and the rest of the friends were already sitting on the big blue bus.

'Do you need some help with the picnic basket?' Levi asked.

Mudroot passed Levi the box of plates and cups. 'If you could take these I can bring the picnic basket.' He smiled. Then he remembered something else. 'Wait there Levi, I just have to fetch a picnic blanket.' Mudroot disappeared to the back of his hut and reappeared a few seconds later with a large red and yellow tartan blanket. 'Now we are all set.' He turned to pick up the picnic hamper and closed his door.

'Don't forget your pickle stick Mudroot.' Levi said.

*

All the friends were squeezed onto the bus. Sebastian was at the front, wearing his drivers cap and taking charge of the large steering wheel.

'We will get there just after eleven thirty.' Sebastian said.

'Good. Just in time for a snack.' Talia smiled.

'Shall we sing a song?' Mudroot looked down the bus.

'Let's sing the wheels on our bus.' Evie called out. 'My baby brother really likes that one.'

'I want to sing a pop song.' Milo shouted out.

'Let's sing the bus song first and then a pop song.' Mudroot said as Evie started them off.

*

The park looked very busy when Sebastian pulled the bus into the car park. There was only one space left for the big blue bus but one space was all that Sebastian needed.

The friends climbed down from the bus and started to carry bags and hampers and boxes over to the picnic area. Mudroot scanned the grassy spot.

'I think we will pitch our blanket over there.'

'Can we go and play?' The harlequin hedgehogs danced around at Mudroot's feet. Mudroot looked down at them and over to the play area. There were swings, a green painted roundabout, a climbing frame, a really big yellow slide, a red see-saw and an activity hut.

'Yes. But be careful. No wandering off. Be back here at one o clock for your lunch.'

The harlequin hedgehogs scurried away quickly, followed by the other animals.

*

Mudroot was lying back on the picnic blanket when he felt a frantic tugging at his coat.

'Mudroot, come quickly. Sebastian is in trouble and all the children are laughing at him.' Milo said.

Mudroot heaved himself up onto his feet and followed Milo towards the play area. He didn't need to walk very far before he spotted Sebastian stuck inside the climbing frame. One of his legs was sticking out between bars, another out of a square shape, another next to the climbing rope and his last leg was planted firmly on the ground with nowhere to go. Sebastian's head poked up out of the top of the climbing frame.

'Ickle fickle what a pickle.' Mudroot said. 'You are a very silly yellow elephant. What have we said about you and the park?' Mudroot scolded.

'Stay away from the climbing frame and the swings.' He stopped. 'I'm very sorry Mudroot but I really like the climbing frame.' Sebastian looked very sad.

'He's too big for the climbing frame.' A little boy said.

'He looks like a big blob of yellow custard.' A little girl laughed. 'Yellow blob, yellow blob, yellow blob.' She chanted as other children joined in.

A fat tear rolled down Sebastian's cheek.

*

ITS ONE O CLOCK MUDROOT

Brian the silver pocket watch shouted out.

This time, instead of making Mudroot jump, Brian makes the little girl, who was calling Sebastian names, jump. She jumped backwards and landed on her bottom. When the other children started to laugh at her the little girl began to cry.

'Ickle fickle what a pickle. Sebastian stuck in the climbing frame. Children who are not very kind and now a little girl crying.'

SORRY I DIDN'T MEAN TO SCARE ANYONE

Brian shouted out, making the little girl stop and look closer.

'Your pocket watch can talk.' She said.

'Yes. His name is Brian.' Mudroot smiled at her. 'Would you like to say hello to him?'

The little girl nodded and walked towards Mudroot.

'Hello Brian.' She smiled.

HELLO.

I HAVE TO GO BACK TO SLEEP!

Brian folded himself back inside Mudroot's waistcoat pocket. The little girl wasn't sure what to do.

'It's okay. Brian is a bit loud and a bit grumpy. He has to be heard you see, to tell us all the time.'

'It's lunch time Mudroot.' Milo said.

'It is lunch time, but first we have to help Sebastian.'

'He is very stuck isn't he?' The little girl said.

'Then we will all have to help unstick him.' Mudroot reached for his pickle stick and pressed it in between Sebastian's foot and one of the bars his foot was stuck in.

A little bit of magic

A tiny tap and click

A few quick dabs

With my magic pickle stick

All the animals and all the children stared as one dab of magical glittery cream slid in between Sebastian's foot and the climbing frame bar, helping the whole foot and leg slide out from the spot it was stuck in.

Mudroot did the same thing for each of the trapped legs and soon Sebastian was free.

The little girl looked, eyes wide. 'Magic!' She smiled.

'Just like magic.' Sebastian smiled.

'I'm sorry for calling you a yellow blob.' The little girl said. 'Come over and meet my mummy and daddy. We can go on the roundabout later.'

'No more roundabouts until after lunch.' Mudroot said. 'Come on, back to the picnic area to have something to eat.'

*

The friends gathered around on the picnic blanket, passing cups and plates and food around. Mudroot looked at the spare cup and plate in his hand.

'Why do I have a spare cup and plate?' He looked around the picnic blanket. Sebastian was sipping some cool lemonade. Buddy and Milo were eating sausage rolls. The harlequin hedgehogs were munching through a bowl of peanuts. Lily and Levi were sharing a bun from the icky sticky bun bush. Sybil swirly snake was sipping dandelion tea. Oscar, the one eyed owl, helped himself to a lollipop from the lollipop tree. Talia and Evie were eating leaf wrapped candy floss. Someone was missing.

'Where is Gwendoline?' Mudroot asked. The friends stop eating and drinking. They looked around. Gwendoline was missing.

*

Mudroot dropped his icky sticky bun and jumped to his feet. 'We have to find Gwendoline. Who was the last one to see her?' He looked at his friends.

'I saw her on the see-saw.' Milo said

'And I saw her playing in the sandpit.' Talia said.

'I was playing hopscotch with her just before lunch.' Lily said.

Have you seen Gwendoline?

'I saw her walking towards the duck pond.' Mara monkey let out a big burp.

BBURRPP!

'Mara!' Mudroot laughed. 'If you drink too much lemonade it makes you burp.'

'I think it was the candy floss.' Mara smiled.

'We will split up into two groups. One group will go to the duck pond and one group will go to the play area.' Mudroot looked at Sebastian. 'Stay away from the climbing frame Sebastian. We don't want you to get stuck again.' He stopped. 'Sebastian can lead the group for the duck pond and I will lead the group for the play area.'

'Don't forget your pickle stick Mudroot.' Oscar, the one-eyed owl, said.

*

Just then Mudroot heard a sound. A singing sound. 'Shush. Can anyone else hear singing?' The friends stopped chattering to listen. 'Yes. We can hear singing.' They said.

'That sounds like Gwendoline.' Sybil said.

This ice cream is free and you don't have to pay
One smile and a rhyme and you're on your way.

She sang her rhyme very slowly with a low, deep voice. Mudroot's pickle stick started to wobble.

'Finally.' He smiled. 'A sign. That is Gwendoline. Let's follow the singing.'

*

Mudroot listened as he heard another rhyme and then a giggle but this time the voice did not belong to Gwendoline. This voice sounded high and squeaky, like it was from a little person.

I like ice-cream, it's the best

But it always makes a mess

The voice giggled and another song danced up to Mudroot's ears.

Strawberry, mint, vanilla too

Three big scoops for me will do

Mudroot walked down the path, with the friends following. They stepped past the trees and the Marigold flowers. Just as they reached the pond, Mudroot spotted a queue of children all lining up for one of Gwendoline's free ice creams.

'Ooh, chocolate ice cream, my favourite.' Oscar chirped as he swooped down to take a large beak full of a cornet, before a little girl had taken one lick. She shrieked and looked up as Oscar flew away.

*

Mudroot walked over to Gwendoline. 'We thought you were lost.' Mudroot said. 'It's past lunch time.'

'I lost track of time and then there was a queue.' Gwendoline looked at Mudroot. 'I can't let the little children down.' She served up another strawberry cornet.

'Then we will bring the picnic to you and take turns to serve ice-cream.' Mudroot said. He tipped his glasses towards Talia to ask for her help in moving the picnic, but his shoes slid onto slippery ice cream and he fell backwards, onto his fat bottom, which let out the loudest fart anyone had ever heard.

TURRUMMP! TURRUMMPP!

Oops! Then another! Where was that noise coming from? Mudroot looked around as all the children started to laugh and although he turned bright red, Mudroot laughed too.

'Come on, let's go and pick up our picnic.'

*

ITS TWO O CLOCK MUDROOT!

Shouted Brian the silver pocket watch.

*

As the clock struck two, the children of Crickleberry town lined up for an ice cream. There were plenty of rhymes and lots of smiles as Gwendoline served the last of her honeycomb vanilla cornets. By the park bench, Mudroot Pickles and his friends started to clear away the empty plates and cups. Sebastian took charge of giving the crockery a quick rinse with his trunk. Mara messy monkey polished off the last nut and swirly Sybil snake swallowed the last of the delicious dandelion tea. The harlequin hedgehogs made a fine job of folding up the picnic blanket and Talia tiger helped Evie and Milo put all of the left-over food, which wasn't very much, back inside the picnic hamper. Buddy blue bear collected the empty lemonade bottles to refill at the lemonade fountain and Levi and Lily, the chocolate spot lions, got ready to carry boxes back to the big blue bus. Oscar, the one-eyed owl, flew above, keeping a look out for any more of his favourite ice creams, even though his belly was already full.

'All aboard the big blue bus.' Mudroot said, leading his friends back to the car park.

.

ITS FOUR O CLOCK MUDROOT!

Shouted Brian the silver pocket watch.

‘We’ll be back in time for tea then.’ Mudroot smiled as he counted his friends back onto the bus and made sure no one was missing.

*

On the way back to Crickleberry Town the friends sang songs and told tall tales about their adventures in the park. Sebastian pretended he was captured by pirates and locked inside the climbing frame dungeon, needing Mudroot’s magic pickle stick to save him. Gwendoline sang about pushing her ice cream cart through a magical forest where the sun shone all day and ice cream was everyone‘s favourite food.

*

With all the friends dropped back to their huts and shacks, Mudroot pulled on his purple silk Pyjamas and settled down in his chair to listen to the radio. It had been another busy day but a wonderful day out at the park.

THE END

Mudroot Pickles' Big Day at School

By

Caroline George

Mudroot Pickles is the big cheese in Crickleberry town. Today he is even more of a big cheese than usual. Mudroot has been asked to cover for Mrs. Pinnybottom at the local school. He feels very, very important fixing his striped bow tie and looking at himself in the mirror.

'What time is it Brian?'

Brian the silver pocket watch grumbled and stretched out his arms. Mudroot had set an alarm for eight o clock and Brian was not happy to be woken up before the alarm.

SOME OF US ARE STILL ASLEEP MUDROOT. IT IS ONLY TWENTY PAST SEVEN IN THE MORNING!

Brian was snappy and grumpy and still tired. He closed his eyes and folded himself back inside Mudroot's waistcoat pocket.

*

As the big cheese in Crickleberry Town, Mudroot Pickles is always the best dressed hedgehog with his bright white shirt fixed with a bow tie and his striped trousers held up with a gold tasseled string. Mudroot pulled on matching striped socks, big and sloppy, that wrinkled over his hairy ankles and adjusted his thick rimmed spectacles. Mudroot reached down into the pocket of his waistcoat to check that Brian, his silver pocket watch, was there. One more brush of his hair, a little raspberry jam to hold it in place and Mudroot was almost ready for his day at school.

Brian shouted out.

ITS EIGHT O CLOCK MUDROOT!

Brian makes him jump. Mudroot falls backwards onto his fat bottom and lets out a loud fart.

TURRUMMP!

'Oops!' Mudroot picked himself up and dusted down his clothes wondering where on earth that silly noise came from. It certainly wasn't from him. He had better not make a habit of falling over today. If he falls over the children and the animals would laugh at him.

*

Today is a very important day because today, Mudroot will be teaching spellings to his class. Mudroot wasn't a very good speller when he went to school. He was always getting his words wrong. But Mudroot only has to help out for one day, unless Mrs Pinnybottom needs to take another day off.

Monday's Mudroot feels so cool

As he sets off to go to school

The bus is full and it's after eight

He'll have to run to not be late.

*

Mudroot pulled on his long purple coat and picked up his satchel. He packed a notepad, pencils a rubber and a pencil sharpener. In the large pocket of his coat he had a packet of mushroom and pickle sandwiches and a bun from the icky sticky bun bush for his lunch.

He stepped outside his front door and bumped into Sebastian the yellow elephant who was cycling to school on his red bicycle.

'Hello Mudroot. Where are you going?' Sebastian asked.

Mudroot waved but hurried on past. 'Can't stop now Sebastian. I am teaching at the school today and I don't want to be late.'

*

Mudroot hurried along the path as Mara raced past on her scooter. 'Hello Mudroot. Where are you going?' Mara asked.

Mudroot waved but hurried on past. 'Can't stop now Mara. I am teaching at the school today and I don't want to be late.'

*

Mudroot crossed the road by the candy floss fence and spotted Levi and Lily heading towards the park.

'Hello Mudroot. Where are you going?' Lily asked.

Mudroot waved but hurried on past. 'Can't stop now Lily. I am teaching at the school today and I don't want to be late.'

*

Mudroot turned down a side street and realised he was lost. He stopped and looked around, recognising the flower shop at the end of the road.

'Ickle fickle what a pickle. I need to be in the next street.' Mudroot doubled back and retraced his steps to find the right street. Now he was going to be late. 'Ickle fickle, ickle fickle' Mudroot muttered to himself.

ITS NINE O CLOCK MUDROOT

Shouted Brian the silver pocket watch.

'Shut up Brian, I am trying to concentrate.' Mudroot snapped, pushing his way in through the double doors of the school.

OH, DO PARDON ME MUDROOT. I'M JUST THE ONE TRYING TO KEEP TIME!

Brian grumped and folded himself back inside the waistcoat pocket.

*

The class were all sat in their seats when Mudroot finally arrived. He sounded a little out of breath, huffing and puffing as he unpacked his satchel. He apologised for being late.

'I was going to offer you a ride on my bicycle.' Sebastian the yellow elephant said.

'And there was plenty of room for you on my scooter.' Mara messy monkey said.

'We always take the shortcut through the park. If you'd walked with us you wouldn't have been late.' Levi the chocolate spot lion said.

'I am here now and that's the main thing.' Mudroot looked a little flustered. He adjusted his glasses and smoothed his hair.

*

'Mrs Pinnybottom told me you have a spelling test today.'

'No.' Chorused the class. 'Mrs Pinnybottom only gives tests on Friday. Today is only Monday.' Sybil swirly snake said.

'I have a note here from Mrs Pinnybottom.' Said Mudroot. 'Spelling test this morning and art this afternoon.'

'Do we have to do a test Mr. Pickles?' Evie looked up.

'Yes you do.' Mudroot pointed at Talia tiger and Milo. 'Come up here and take this paper and these pencils. Give everyone a sheet of paper and a pencil.'

*

Mudroot walked back and forth in front of the blackboard as Milo and Talia handed out the paper and pencils.

'Write your name on top of the sheet of paper and then we will start the test.'

'Can I have a rubber in case I make a mistake.' Oscar, the one eyed owl, asked. He was very good at flying and eating ice cream but he wasn't very good at spelling. Mudroot opened the drawer of Mrs Pinnybottom's desk and pulled out a spare rubber.

'Here you go Oscar.'

'Can I have a pencil sharpener please Mr. Pickles. My pencil is blunt.' Buddy blue bear asked. Mudroot opened the drawer of Mrs Pinnybottom's desk again and pulled out a spare pencil sharpener.

'Here you go Buddy.'

*

Mudroot watched as his class buried their heads in paper to write their names at the top of their sheets. All of the class were able to spell their own names. Mudroot lifted up the piece of paper that Mrs. Pinnybottom left for him. All the words were five letter words and Mudroot had the sheet with all the correct spellings written down on it. That was a relief. Mudroot wasn't very good at spellings.

*

'Number one. Spell green.' Mudroot rattled through the list. He could spell green easily enough but he wasn't so sure about a couple of the other words. 'Last word. Spell glove.'

ITS TEN O CLOCK MUDROOT

Shouted Brian who stayed outside the waistcoat pocket this time in hope of a snack.

Mudroot was sitting down in the schoolteachers chair so he didn't fall or fart. His day was already getting better.

DO YOU HAVE ANY CRISPS MUDROOT?

Brian shouted out.

Mudroot stuffed his hand inside his coat pocket and pulled out a chocolate biscuit.

'This is all for now. Don't get crumbs everywhere. I have a class to teach today.' Mudroot said.

Brian took the chocolate biscuit and disappeared inside the waistcoat pocket.

*

'Leave all of your papers on your desk and I will collect them.' Mudroot looked at his sheet of paper with all the correct spellings on it and set it down on his chair. He walked in between the rows of desks and picked up all the test papers.

'I will have them all marked after lunch.' Mudroot sat down in his chair, forgetting that his sheet of spellings had been left on the top of it.

Silly Mudroot!

'Now we are going to go around the class to pick up some more of that story about the witch and her cat.' Mudroot opened up a story book.

*

Mara messy monkey is the only student in class who did not know when playtime had finished and reading had begun. She was fidgeting in her chair and throwing small pieces of paper at the other students. Mara climbed off her chair and then climbed up on it again. Then she sat on her desk saying it was more comfortable than her chair. Mudroot felt exhausted watching her, telling her to sit still.

Another small ball of paper landed on his desk and Mudroot noticed how Mara ducked behind Gwendoline and started to chuckle.

'Mara monkey. That is enough.' Mudroot slammed his pickle stick down on the floor.' Sit still and read.'

'Mara doesn't mean it Mr. Pickles' said Evie. 'She just gets a little bit fizzy after playtime.'

'Fizzy? She's a monkey not a bottle of lemonade from the lemonade fountain.' Said Mudroot.

'Mrs Pinnybottom lets Mara sit up front on her desk until she stops being so fizzy.' Said Milo.

'Come up here and sit with me then Mara.' Mudroot waved her over to him, ignoring her cartwheels through the row of desks. 'Sit quietly with your book or I might have to send you out into the corridor.' He looked sternly at her through his glasses.'

'Not the corridor.' Gasped the other students. 'Mrs Blockchop will find her.'

'Mrs Blockchop the headteacher?' Mudroot looked at his class who all nodded. Mudroot felt a little scared of Mrs Blockchop too. She was the head teacher when Mudroot was at school. Mrs Blockchop never smiled and never ever found anything funny.

'Then Mara, you had better behave yourself.' Mudroot said.

ITS TWELVE O CLOCK MUDROOT

Shouted Brian the silver pocket watch.

'Okay class. It is lunchtime. After lunch I will tell you how you all did with your spelling tests.'

Mudroot sat behind his desk, wondering why none of his students seem keen to move, except Mara.

'Off you go. Have some lunch.'

'We don't like the school dinners Mr. Pickles. Most of us have brought in our own sandwiches.' Oscar, the one eyed owl, pulled out a bread roll from underneath his wing.

'Not like school dinners? When I was a young hedgehog, school dinners were my favourite part of the day. Creamy mashed potato, treacle pudding with custard.' Mudroot licked his lips, wishing he had more than a mushroom and pickle sandwich to enjoy.

'The food is rubbish here unless you like burgers and chips.' Said Buddy pulling out his lunchbox and opening it up at his desk.

'You all like burger and chips.' Mudroot smiled.

'Not every day.' Said Talia biting into a green apple.

'Then you'll have to take your sandwiches out to the playground. I have test papers to mark.' Mudroot looked at them, itching to unwrap his own lunch.

*

After finishing his sandwich and washing it down with some water from the dispenser in the hall, Mudroot searched through the papers on his desk for the answer sheet. It was nowhere to be found.

'Ickle fickle what a pickle. How will I know if the spellings are right?' He looked through the papers again. No luck. Mudroot reached for his magic pickle stick and started to chant quietly.

Here I am at the head of the class

Trying to mark them all with a pass

Without the answers I fear I am stuck

I hope my pickle stick can bring me luck

*

Mudroot walked out into the playground and interrupted the harlequin hedgehogs who were playing hopscotch.

'Hello Mr Pickles.' They smiled. 'Would you like to play hopscotch?'

'Not today harlequins. I am looking for a sheet of paper with spellings on it. Have you seen it anywhere?' Mudroot asked.

The harlequins shook their heads. ‘No. Sorry Mr Pickles.’

Mudroot turned away and thought he could hear the harlequins laughing. He shook his head. They couldn’t be laughing at him.

*

Mudroot walked past the bicycle shed where Sebastian, Buddy and Talia were finishing their lunch.

‘Hello Mr Pickles.’ They smiled. ‘Did you enjoy your lunch?’

‘I did thank you. I am looking for a sheet of paper with spellings on it. Have you seen it anywhere?’ Mudroot asked.

The friends shook their heads. ‘No. Sorry Mr Pickles.’

Mudroot turned away and thought he could hear Sebastian the yellow elephant chuckle. He shook his head. Sebastian couldn't be laughing at him.

*

Mudroot walked past the sports hall where Lily and Evie were playing catch.

'Hello Mr Pickles.' They smiled. 'Do you want to play?'

'No thank you. I am looking for a sheet of paper with spellings on it. Have you seen it anywhere?' Mudroot asked.

The friends shook their heads. 'No. Sorry Mr Pickles.'

Mudroot turned away and thought he could hear Lily and Evie giggle. He shook his head. They couldn't be laughing at him.

*

Just then Mudroot heard Gwendoline giraffe, who always brought her ice cream cart into school. Gwendoline was standing by the woodwork room.

This ice cream is free and you don't have to pay
One smile and a rhyme and you're on your way.

She sang her rhyme very slowly with a low, deep voice. 'Hello Mr Pickles. Do you have a rhyme for me?'

No ice cream, I've had plenty to eat
But can you help find my answer sheet?

'I'm very sorry but I haven't seen it. Why not have one of these lovely honeycomb ices instead.'

'No thanks Gwendoline, not today.'

Mudroot walked back to his classroom, ignoring the giggles from Gwendoline and wondering where on earth the answer sheet was. He had looked everywhere. On the desk, in his bag, underneath the books and he had even walked around the playground asking his friends where it was.

He sat down on his wooden chair and heard a rustle of paper. Quickly he stood up and turned his head around to look behind him. There it was. The spelling paper was stuck to the back of his coat, right by his bottom.

That's what they were all laughing at. There he was, asking them if they had seen a sheet of paper, and all this time it was stuck to his bottom. The joke was on him. Mudroot turned red as he sat down and started to mark the test.

ITS ONE O CLOCK MUDROOT!

Shouted Brian the silver pocket watch.

*

As the clock struck one, the students returned to the classroom, their chatter slowing down as they took their seats.

'You will all be pleased to hear that I found the answer sheet and so I was able to mark your spelling tests.' He paused. 'You all did very well. Mrs Pinnybottom expected you all to get at least six right and all of you got eight or more correct spellings. Well done.' He walked through the rows of desks handing back the spelling tests to the students. 'The writing in green ink is the correct spelling for the words you may have got wrong this time.' He smiled. 'So, who is ready for arts and crafts?'

*

The afternoon in Crickleberry town's school was spent making raffia baskets, plasticine models and glitter pictures. Buddy blue bear ended up covered in glitter and Levi had plasticine stuck in his mane but none of it mattered. There was lots of chatting as Gwendoline the giraffe served ice cream as a treat for doing so well in the spelling test.

*

With school finally closed for the day Mudroot pulled on his purple silk Pyjamas and switched off his light. It had been another busy day but a wonderful day at school.

THE END

Mudroot Pickles & The Rainy Day

By

Caroline George

As the big cheese in Crickleberry Town, Mudroot Pickles is the best dressed hedgehog. He wears a bright white shirt fixed with a bow tie and a pair of green trousers held up with a gold tasseled string. Mudroot loves his bow ties; tartan, striped and even spots. Mudroot has matching socks, big and sloppy, that wrinkled over his hairy ankles and because Mudroot is a very important hedgehog, he wears thick rimmed spectacles and has a mustard colour waistcoat where he keeps Brian, his silver pocket watch.

Brian shouts out the time to Mudroot whenever the clock strikes the hour. Sometimes,

Brian can be grumpy, especially if Mudroot disturbs him to ask for the time. Grumpy old Brian!

*

Today it was raining in Crickleberry Town, weather that even a magic pickle stick had no control over. Mudroot Pickles hated the rain. When it rained it meant he could not ride his motorbike and he had to cover up his fantastic socks with wellington boots. More than that the rain made all of his friends miserable too.

*

Brian shouted out.

ITS TEN O CLOCK MUDROOT!

Brian makes him jump. Mudroot falls backwards onto his fat bottom and lets out a loud fart.

TURRUMMP!

'Oops!' Mudroot picked himself up and dusted down his clothes wondering where on earth that silly noise came from. It certainly wasn't from him.

*

Buddy blue bear leaned out of his window, one paw resting under his chin. It was raining. This was not a good day. He put on his red anorak and wellington boots and walked to Mudroot's hut, past the jelly bean carousel and the icky sticky bun bush. He knocked on Mudroot's front door.

'Hello Buddy.' Mudroot smiled, opening the door. 'Not a very nice day for a walk is it?'

'I'm bored. What can I do?'

Mudroot scratched his head. 'I don't know Buddy. What would you like to do?'

The blue bear shrugged. He was bored but he had no idea what to do to entertain himself.

*

There was another knock at the door.

'Hello Sebastian.' Mudroot smiled, opening his door. 'Not a very nice day for a walk is it?'

'I'm bored. What can I do?'

Mudroot scratched his head. 'I don't know Sebastian. What would you like to do?'

The yellow elephant sighed. He was bored but had no idea what to do to entertain himself.

*

There was another knock at the door.

Mudroot looked around his hut that was getting very full up with just two visitors.

'Hello Lily. Hello Levi.' Mudroot smiled, opening his door. 'Not a very nice day for a walk is it?'

'We're bored. What can we do?'

Mudroot scratched his head. 'I don't know Lily, Levi. What would you like to do?'

The chocolate spot lions sighed. They were bored but had no idea what to do to entertain themselves.

*

Brian shouted out.

ITS ELEVEN O CLOCK MUDROOT!

Brian made him jump. Mudroot falls backwards onto his fat bottom and lets out a loud fart.

TURRUMMP!

'Oops!' Mudroot picked himself up and dusted down his clothes wondering where on earth that silly noise came from. It certainly wasn't from him.

*

'I have an idea.' Mudroot looked at his friends as the animals looked back at him. 'Why don't we all go to the old barn. There's bound to be something for us to do there.' Mudroot suggested.

'It's full of old stuff.' Sebastian said.

'If I remember correctly' Mudroot said, reaching for his pickle stick, 'there are jigsaw puzzles and board games in the barn. Maybe we can find something to play with.' He tapped his pickle stick on the floor hoping to magic up some entertainment.

*

'Come on. Put your coats back on and we'll go to the barn.' He looked at Levi. 'Why don't you round up the others. I'm sure they are all just as bored as we are.'

Mudroot pulled on his wellington boots and joined his friends out in the garden. Levi had already walked on ahead to find the others.

'Come on. We'll have to walk quickly or we will all get soaked.' Mudroot marched on ahead.

*

'Look Mudroot. 'There's Evie stood by her red bicycle. It looks like she is crying. Maybe she has fallen off and hurt herself.' Sebastian said.

'Hello Evie.' Said Mudroot. 'What's the matter?'

'My bicycle is stuck in the mud and I can't get home.'

'Sebastian can use his trunk to lift your bicycle out of the mud but you can't cycle home in this. You'll only get stuck again.' Mudroot paused. 'Why don't you come to the barn with us. We're going to play some games.'

'Can Sebastian bring my bicycle please? I don't want to leave it out in the rain.'

Sebastian curled his trunk around the handlebars of Evie's bicycle and hoisted it up.

'Yes, I can bring your bicycle.' He smiled.

*

Mudroot pulled out a bunch of keys from his coat pocket and searched through the silver and gold keys for the one that opened the lock to the barn door.

'Here it is.' He held up a long silver key and put it inside the lock. One turn, two turns and a click. Mudroot pushed open the barn door just as Levi joined them with Sybil swirly snake, Gwendoline giraffe, Oscar, the one eyed owl, Mara messy monkey and the harlequin hedgehogs in tow.

*

'Where is Talia?' Mudroot looked at Levi.

'She's not feeling very well. She has decided to stay in her shack.'

'What's wrong with her?' Mudroot looked worried.

'She thinks she may have eaten too much ice cream.'

'Oh dear.' Mudroot said.

'She will need some of your magic medicine Mudroot. ' Mara said.

Mudroot stopped taking off his coat and started to put it back on. 'Why don't you all start looking inside those boxes for something to do and I'll go and get some magic medicine for Talia.'

*

'Shall I come and help?' Came a small voice they had not heard for a while.

'Hello Milo.' Mudroot smiled. 'What are you doing here?'

'I was hoping to get some lemonade and then I saw Levi so I followed him.' He looked up. 'If Talia is sick then she will need to see the doctor.' He looked down at the doctors bag he brought with him. 'I'm the doctor so I will be able to help.' Milo smiled.

'What a good idea. Come with me Milo and we'll go and look after Talia.'

*

Gwendoline was the first to open a box, pushing her nose inside and rummaging through the books that were packed inside.

'We can read some stories.' She pulled out a book about dancing.

'Boring.' Mara said as she rummaged inside another box. 'What about a jigsaw puzzle?'

'Where are we going to put it?' Lily looked at her. 'The floor is all bumpy and there isn't a table. You need a flat surface to join the pieces.'

'There are some building bricks here.' Levi said, tipping over a box of multi coloured wooden blocks. 'We can see who can build the tallest tower without it falling over.'

'You need a flat surface for that too silly.' Lily looked at him.

'We can build it on top of one of Gwendoline's story books.' Levi said.

*

Buddy shook his head. 'I don't want to build with wooden blocks. Isn't there something else to do.'

'What's inside that box next to you.' One of the harlequin hedgehogs asked.

Buddy opened up the lid and peered inside. 'It looks like those board games Mudroot was talking about.' He pulled out a game of snakes and ladders.

'Sybil's game.' Sybil smiled at the snakes on the outside of the box.

'There's also a draughts board and some playing cards.' Buddy smiled. 'We could play Happy Families.'

'Are there any other card games. Those pictures of Mr Bones the doctor always scare me.' Lily said.

'There is a pack of ordinary playing cards, red ones and black ones. We can play snap.'

'Card games will be over too quickly.' Sebastian said.

*

'Got it.' Oscar flew above the group and dropped a wizards hat down on top of Mara's head. 'There's a dressing up box at the back, full of different costumes. Why don't we all dress up before Mudroot and Milo come back and they can judge the winner.'

'What's the prize?' One of the harlequin hedgehogs looked up.

‘I haven’t got that far. Maybe Mudroot can think of a prize.’

*

Mudroot stopped off at his hut on his way to Talia’s shack to pick up some magic medicine. It wasn’t anything more than a tub of treacle with glitter sprinkles but somehow did the trick when Mara complained of tummy ache. He passed the pot to Milo.

‘You should probably put this inside your doctors bag for our visit today. Far better for the doctor to give the medicine.’ He ruffled the little boy’s hair.

‘I’ve got bandages too and my thermometer.’ Milo smiled, putting the magic medicine inside his bag.

*

Talia tiger was tucked up in bed with a hot water bottle feeling very sorry for herself when Mudroot and Milo arrived.

'We heard you might be needing to see a doctor.' Mudroot smiled. 'And luckily for you Dr. Milo was in the area.'

Talia managed a small smile but it was clear she was feeling poorly. She moved slightly and let out a small moan in pain.

'Ickle, fickle what a pickle. Poorly Talia and all this rain.' Mudroot muttered, tapping his magic pickle stick on the ground. 'Come on pickle stick, time to make Talia better and put a stop to this rain.'

'I think I need some magic medicine.' Talia groaned.

Milo opened his doctors bag. 'I need to take your temperature first Talia.' He waved his plastic thermometer in front of her head. 'Open wide.' Talia opened her mouth and Milo placed the thermometer under her tongue. He looked at Mudroot. 'What time is it please Mudroot?'

Brian shouted out, grumbling about being woken up earlier than expected.

ITS TWENTY FIVE PAST ELEVEN MUDROOT!

Brian makes him jump. Mudroot falls backwards onto his fat bottom and lets out a loud fart.

TURRUMMP!

'Oops!' Mudroot picked himself up and dusted down his clothes wondering where on earth that silly noise came from. It certainly wasn't from him.

Milo chuckled. 'I just have to leave the thermometer in for one minute and then we can decide what to do.'

*

Talia stayed perfectly still while Milo checked the reading on his thermometer.

'You have a tummy ache and will need some magic medicine.' Dr. Milo reached inside his bag and pulled out the jar that Mudroot gave him.

'I hope that's magic medicine.' Talia looked at him as Dr. Milo opened the jar and stuck a spoon into the sludge.

'Yes. Magic medicine.' He said, showing her the spoonful of glittering paste.

Talia opened up her mouth and licked her lips after the first spoonful.

'I'll have to put a plaster on your tummy too. That will help it to feel better.' Dr. Milo pulled back Talia's blanket and stuck a spotty plaster on her belly. 'There. All done. I will come and check on you tomorrow but you should start to feel better soon.' Dr. Milo smiled.

Brian shouted out.

ITS TWELVE O CLOCK MUDROOT!

Brian makes Mudroot jump but this time Mudroot is sat on a chair so does not fall backwards or let any loud noises escape from his bottom.

'Twelve o clock already. This is good news. Almost halfway through the rainy day and hopefully our friends will have found something to do in the barn'.

*

The barn was upside down by the time Mudroot and Milo returned from Talia's shack. There was lots of noise and material flying around everywhere. Wizards hats, broomsticks, Roman helmets and shields. One of the harlequin hedgehogs was dressed up as a gladiator and another dressed as one of the seven dwarves.

'We found the dressing up box.' Oscar, the one eyed owl, flew above them sporting an Indian headdress and carrying a bow and arrow.

'Once we are all changed, you and Milo can be the judges.'

'You've been busy.' Mudroot smiled, pleased his friends found something to do.

*

Mudroot sat down on one of the boxes watching with a smile as his friends swapped costumes. Sybil poked her head out of the dressing up box covered in beaded necklaces.

'There is some make-up at the bottom of the box, lipsticks, eyeshadow and even a fake beard and moustache if anyone is interested.' She hissed.

*

Lily the chocolate spot lion tapped Mudroot on the arm.

'Evie hurt her finger when she fell off her bicycle. I said that Dr. Milo would look at it.'

'Dr. Milo.' Mudroot called. 'You have another patient.'

Evie stood in front of Mudroot and Mio and stuck her finger underneath their noses. It was just a teeny, tiny, scratch but there was some blood.

'I don't think it's going to fall off.' Dr. Milo looked at Mudroot for a second opinion.

'Heavens no.' Mudroot held up his pickle stick and started to chant.

A little bit of magic

A tiny tap and click

A few quick dabs

With my magic pickle stick.

Evie stared as one dab of magical glittery cream soothed her grazed finger.

'Magic!' She smiled.

'Just like magic.' Mudroot smiled as Dr. Milo wrapped a spotty plaster around the sore finger.

'Thank you, Dr. Milo. Now I think we have a fancy dress competition to judge.' Mudroot said.

ITS TWO O CLOCK MUDROOT!

Shouted Brian the silver pocket watch.

*

As the clock struck two, the animals of Crickleberry town lined up behind the bales of hay in the barn ready to show off their fine costumes. Mudroot and Milo sat on boxes of books and games, ready to judge.

Sybil Swirly snake was first, dressed as a hula hula dancer with a feather boa, lots of necklaces and a pineapple for a hat. Messy Mara monkey proudly strutted out from the hay, dressed as a pirate complete with bandana and swashbuckling sword.

Next came the harlequin hedgehogs dressed in Roman robes with the last hedgehog dressed as a gladiator. Buddy blue bear followed, playing his banjo and dressed as a clown complete with a comedy red nose that tooted when he squeezed it. Next to Buddy, came Sebastian the yellow elephant dressed as an American football player. Levi and Lily lion opted for a double act, dressed as the king and queen of Crickleberry town with long robes and sparkling crowns.

Oscar, the one-eyed owl, flew above, dressed as an Indian warrior with extra feathers and his bow and arrow. But, the stars of the show were

Gwendoline and Evie who dressed as a double act, Aladdin riding in on a very tall unicorn.

*

Brian the silver pocket watch shouted out again.

ITS FOUR O CLOCK MUDROOT

Mudroot stood up and looked at Evie and Milo.

'It must be time for you two to make your way back home.' He opened the barn door, delighted to see that the rain had stopped and sun shining behind a beautiful rainbow. The two children waved and set off back to town.

*

With all the fancy dress costumes returned to their box at the back of the barn, Mudroot had his eye on a nice mushroom pie for tea. As the friends made their way back to their own homes, Mudroot thought of his pie, his bed and his purple silk Pyjamas. It had been another busy day but a wonderful fancy dress parade on a rainy day.

THE END

Mudroot Pickles & The Christmas Visitor

by

Caroline George

As the big cheese in Crickleberry Town, Mudroot Pickles is the best dressed hedgehog. With Christmas just around the corner Mudroot swapped his bright white shirt for a green and white striped jumper, with a pocket on the front for Brian, his shouty silver pocket watch.

It was very cold today and when Mudroot looked out of his window he could see lots of snow on the ground. Brian, the silver pocket watch, yawned and stretched.

ITS EIGHT O CLOCK MUDROOT

Mudroot was still staring out of the window. His motorbike was almost covered in snow and as Buddy blue bear walked past his house, he was neck deep in the white flakes.

Buddy looked across and waved. 'Hello Mudroot. Are you going to help us build a snowman today?' He stopped outside Mudroot's hut.

Mudroot opened his window, just a little. It was very cold and Mudroot did not want to let all of that cold air inside his warm, toasty hut.

'Maybe later. I haven't had my breakfast yet.' He called out and closed his window. That was enough fresh air for now.

*

With a big plate of hot buttered toast and a mug of dandelion tea, Mudroot sat by his fire warming his toes. He was wearing his favourite red and white striped sloppy socks and he also had his tartan slippers on, but his toes still felt a little bit cold. He took another bite of toast, thinking about his bobble hat, scarf and gloves. He would need to wrap himself up very well indeed if he was going to help build a snowman.

There was a knock on his door. A quick, urgent sounding rappity rap. Mudroot moved away from his fire and opened the door. It was Sebastian the yellow elephant.

'You have to come quickly. Someone is in the barn.'

'Who is in the barn?' Mudroot sounded surprised. 'The barn is locked.'

Sebastian started to shake and tremble. 'I don't know. I was on my way to meet Buddy to build a snowman when I heard a noise coming from the barn. I was too scared to look inside.'

'What sort of noise was it?' Mudroot looked at the trembling elephant.

Sebastian gave a shrug. 'Dunno.'

Mudroot finished his tea and toast and pulled on his long red coat. Sebastian could be a silly billy sometimes. It was probably just some birds flapping about in the barn. Mudroot reached for his spotty bobble hat and put it on his head, watching himself in his mirror to make sure that he didn't spoil his hair. Then he wrapped a striped scarf around his neck and pushed his hands inside his thick woolen mittens.

'Right then Sebastian. Let's see who is in the barn.'

'Don't forget your pickle stick.' Sebastian pointed to the magic stick leaning up by the chair.

*

The friends walked past the licorice lamp posts and stopped by the icky sticky bun bush where Levi and Lily the chocolate spot lions were standing, both wrapped up in brightly coloured knitwear.

'Hello Mudroot. Hello Sebastian. Are you going to help Buddy build a snowman?'

'Yes we are but first we need to find out who is in the barn.' Mudroot said.

'Who's in the barn?' Lily asked.

'We don't know but whoever it is has frightened Sebastian so we are going to have a look.'

'We'll come with you.' Said Levi, puffing out his chest.

*

The four friends walked up to the lemonade fountain where Evie and Milo were filling up bottles to drink later. Evie was dressed head to toe in a navy blue padded ski suit with boots to match. She had a bright pink bobble hat on with matching gloves. Milo was dressed in his green anorak, dark jeans and wellington boots. No bobble hat but a pair of black fluffy ear muffs, a striped scarf and a pair of brown gloves. They both looked very warm.

'Hello Mudroot. Hello Sebastian. Hello Levi. Hello Lily. Are you going to help Buddy build a snowman?' Evie smiled.

'Yes we are but first we need to find out who is in the barn.' Mudroot said.

'Who's in the barn?' Milo asked.

'We don't know but whoever it is frightened Sebastian so we are going to have a look.'

'We'll come with you.' Said Evie and Milo, stuffing the bottles of lemonade inside back packs.

*

The six friends walked up to Gwendoline who was shivering by the side of her ice cream cart.

This i-i-ice cream is f-f-f-ree and you d-d-don't have to p-p-pay

One s-s-smile and a rh-h-hyme and you're o-o-n your w-w-way

'Hello Gwendoline. No thank you. It's far too cold for ice-cream today.' Mudroot looked at her. Gwendoline had on her woolen hat, her red scarf and two pairs of red socks on her feet. It wasn't enough to keep her warm. 'Where is your wooly poncho?

'I left it in the barn and when I went to get it, I could hear strange noises coming from inside.'

'Who was inside the barn?' Evie asked.

'I didn't look. I was too scared.'

'Come with us Gwendoline. We are going to the barn to take a look. We can find out who is in the barn together and you can pick up your poncho.' Mudroot said.

ITS NINE O CLOCK MUDROOT

Brian shouted out, making Mudroot jump. Mudroot fell backwards onto his fat bottom and let out a loud fart.

TURRUMMP!

Oops! Mudroot picked himself up and dusted down his clothes, wondering where on earth that silly noise was coming from. It certainly wasn't from him.

*

Mudroot tapped his pickle stick on the ground.

Today is Friday, we have a guest
Our barn is just the place to rest
We'll make our way to check it out
And make a snowman with a perfect snout

The seven friends walked closer to the candy floss fence where Talia Tiger and Mara messy monkey were rolling up snowballs.

'Hello Mudroot. Hello Sebastian. Hello Levi. Hello Lily. Hello Milo. Hello Evie. Hello Gwendoline. Are you going to help Buddy build a snowman?' Talia smiled.

'Yes we are but first we need to find out who is in the barn.' Mudroot said.

'Who's in the barn?' Mara asked.

'We don't know but whoever it is frightened Sebastian and they have Gwendoline's poncho so we are going to have a look.'

'We'll come with you.' Said Talia and Mara, dropping snowballs into a box.

*

The nine friends walked up to the lollipop tree where Sybil swirly snake was easing her body into a long woolen sock. She curled her body down the tree and looked at the group of friends.

'Hello Sybil.' Mudroot smiled.

'Good morning to you all. Are you going to help Buddy build a snowman?' Sybil put on her blue bobble hat.

'Yes we are but first we need to find out who is in the barn.' Mudroot said.

'Who's in the barn?' Sybil asked as Oscar, the one eyed owl, flew above.

'We don't know but whoever it is frightened Sebastian and they have Gwendoline's poncho so we are going to have a look.'

'Whoever it is took half of my winter supply of berries and nuts.' Oscar frowned.

'Then you had better come with us.' Said Mudroot, leading the way towards the barn.

*

As the friends approached the barn Mudroot raised his pickle stick and came to a stop.

'Shush. Listen.' Mudroot leaned his ear closer to the barn door and his friends did the same.

ITS TEN O CLOCK MUDROOT

Brian shouted out and made Mudroot almost jump out of his red coat. He falls backwards, onto his fat bottom, letting out the loudest fart anyone has ever heard.

TURRUMMP! TURRUMMPP!

Oops! Then another! Where was that noise coming from? It certainly wasn't from him. Mudroot stood up and dusted down his red coat. He leaned in closer to the barn door and listened again.

CRACKLE. BRUSH. STAMP. GRUMBLE.

‘What is that?’ Sebastian trembled. ‘It’s not a yellow elephant.’

‘It doesn’t sound like a lion.’ Lily says.

CRACKLE. BRUSH. STAMP. GRUMBLE.

‘It’s not a tiger or a monkey.’ Said Milo.

`Is it a cow?’ Evie asked.

‘Maybe it is a dinosaur.’ Said Mara. These woods are very, very old.’

'There are no dinosaurs here.' Said Mudroot as Sebastian shrank back, his bobble hat wobbling on his head.

'Someone will have to go inside and take a look?' Said Lily.

'I'm not going in there.' Said Sebastian.

'I d-d-don't w-w-want to go in either, even if I r-r-really n-n-need my p-p-poncho.' Said Gwendoline.

'Ickle fickle what a pickle. This is turning out to be a pretty scary day. I guess I will have to go inside and take a look.' said Mudroot. He stepped forward, very slowly and very quietly, thinking he could get close enough to peep around the side of the door. Suddenly his magic pickle stick started to vibrate and there was a loud noise from inside the barn.

HO! HO! HO!

Mudroot jumped out of his skin, falling backwards into the snow again, landing on his fat bottom and letting out a big fart.

TURRUMMP!

Where was that noise coming from? It certainly wasn't from him. Mudroot stood back up and dusted down his red coat. He leaned in closer to the barn door and listened again.

HO! HO! HO!

Came the sound again.

‘I know who that is.’ Evie gasped, her eyes wide and shining with excitement. Evie raced past Mudroot and into the barn. ‘It’s Santa Claus.’ She laughed, running into the barn with the rest of her friends following her in.

There, resting underneath Gwendoline’s poncho by the bales of hay lay two reindeers. Beside them, a half-eaten bowl of berries.

‘My winter supplies.’ Said Oscar, perching on the end of a bale of hay.

‘My poncho.’ said Gwendoline.

HO! HO! HO! AND WHO DO WE HAVE HERE?

Santa Claus smiled at the group of friends as Evie did her very best to make all the introductions.

'Sebastian was a little scared when he heard noises coming from the barn.' She said.

'I'm very sorry to have scared you Sebastian.' Said Santa Claus. 'We were just flying over Crickleberry town, on our way to Australia, when Rummer knocked her hoof on a chimney pot.' He looked at Rummer. 'We needed somewhere to rest and your barn was perfect.'

'My foot was very sore.' Rummer said, licking a small cut at the bottom of her hoof.

'You didn't stop because you were hungry then.' Said Oscar, eyeing the half-eaten bowl of his winter berries.

HO! HO! HO!

Santa laughed. 'That was me little owl. I am always hungry.'

'That's why we leave out plenty of cookies and milk on Christmas Eve.' Milo said.

'And carrots for the reindeer.'

Ruby the reindeer snorted. 'I prefer fairy cakes to carrots.'

'So do I.' Evie laughed.

'You didn't stop because you were cold?' Said Gwendoline, looking at her poncho draped over Rummer and Ruby.

HO! HO! HO!

Santa chuckled. 'That was me too. I saw the pretty poncho and thought it might stop Rummer from thinking about her sore foot.' He looked at

Gwendoline who stood shivering inside the barn and lifted up the poncho. 'Here you are Gwendoline. The straw will keep Rummer and Ruby warm. You put your poncho on.' He smiled as Milo walked past him with his doctors bag.

'I didn't know you had a doctor here.' Santa looked surprised as Milo opened his bag.

*

Milo kneeled down beside Rummer and put his stethoscope onto her chest, listening to her breathing.

'That all sounds okay to me Rummer. Now I need to take your temperature.' He pushed his plastic thermometer underneath Rummer's tongue and looked at her poorly foot. 'It's just a small scratch but you'll need a plaster and a bandage.' Milo spoke very seriously as he removed the thermometer. He looked at the reading. 'Very good.' He smiled and wrapped her foot in a bandage.

'Thank you Milo.' Said Santa Claus. 'You have saved Christmas eve.'

'Shouldn't you be delivering presents?' Evie looked at him.

'Yes I should and I'd like to start with you and your friends.' Santa Claus smiled and walked behind the bales of hay, returning with a large red sack. 'Put your foot inside there Sebastian and pull out a Christmas gift.'

Sebastian dipped his foot inside the bag and curled his toes around a present. He pulled out a box wrapped in blue and red paper with a yellow bow.

'Can I open it now?' He looked at Santa Claus.

'What do your friends say? I know it's only Christmas Eve and presents should not be opened until Christmas day but...' He looked at Mudroot.

'This is such a special occasion I think it's perfectly fine to open presents now.' Mudroot smiled.

As the friends dipped inside Santa's sack and pulled out lots of amazing gifts, Mudroot was distracted. He had forgotten something but he couldn't remember what.

ITS TWO O CLOCK MUDROOT

Brian the silver pocket watch shouted out.

'I have something in my sack for Brian too.' Santa walked across to Mudroot and held the sack open in front of Brian who reached in and pulled out a small box. Brian started to rip off the paper and clapped his hands as he pulled out his very own set of winter knitwear.

'Something to keep you warm when you pop up to tell the time.' Santa smiled.

*

All of the friends were delighted with their gifts. There was a new scooter for Mara, matching Pyjamas for Levi and Lily, a gold framed mirror for Sybil, roller skates for Gwendoline and lots of other wonderful presents. Santa looked at Mudroot who was still admiring his new emerald green coat.

'These presents are for your other friends, the harlequin hedgehogs and Buddy blue bear.' He handed Mudroot some more boxes.

'Oh no. I forgot about Buddy. Ickle fickle what a pickle. We were all supposed to be helping Buddy build a snowman.'

'We still have time to help Buddy.' Sebastian said.

Mudroot looked at Santa Claus. 'Will you be okay here in the barn?'

Santa stood up. 'Now that Rummer's foot is all better we'd best be making a move. We need to go back to the workshop and pick up some more presents. Thank you Dr. Milo. Thank you all.'

'Where is your sleigh Santa?' Evie asked.

'It's around the back of the barn. Would you like to see it and meet my other reindeers before we fly away?'

*

As Santa and his sleigh prepared to leave Crickleberry town, Mudroot Pickles and his friends headed back through the woodland to find Buddy. As they approached the park, all they could see were lots of snowmen. Small ones, big ones. Snowmen wearing silly hats, some with scarves and gloves.

'There you are. We were beginning to think you weren't coming.' Buddy padded towards Mudroot as two of the harlequin hedgehogs placed a scarf around the last snowman.

'We got side tracked by Santa Claus and his reindeer.' Mudroot said.

Buddy laughed. 'Santa Claus? You'll have to do better than that Mudroot. Everyone knows that Santa Claus is very busy on Christmas eve.'

'Look up.' Mudroot smiled.

'Happy Christmas Buddy blue bear. Happy Christmas Harlequin hedgehogs. Happy Christmas all of you. Enjoy your presents. **HO! HO! HO!**' Santa and his sleigh vanished into the afternoon clouds just as more snow started to fall.

*

With Christmas eve saved and all of his friends tucked up for the night, Mudroot pulled on his red silk Pyjamas and switched off his light. It had been another busy but wonderful day. Tomorrow, with a Christmas day feast and lots of presents it would be just as busy.

THE END

Printed in France by Amazon
Brétigny-sur-Orge, FR

16152811R00120